KARMA
UNRAVELLED

Published by Gurumaa Vani

Registered Office:
57, Ajanta Apartments
36, I.P.Extension, Patparganj
Delhi - 110 092, India
info@gurumaa.com

First Published in India by Gurumaa Vani, 2014
Copyright© 2014 Gurumaa Vani
All rights reserved.

ISBN 978-93-81464-39-7

Translated & Compiled by Dr. Urmila Pandey

No part of this book may be reproduced or
transmitted in any form or by any means
electronic or mechanical including photocopying
or recording or by any information storage and
retrieval system without permission
in writing from the publisher.

KARMA UNRAVELLED

Anandmurti Gurumaa

Contents

INTRODUCTION

No rational being would deny the well-established laws of Physics. Whether it is Newton's laws of motion, law of gravity or Einstein's theory of relativity – such laws have universal acceptance. What's more, even if anyone was daft enough to say I don't believe in gravity, the force of gravity would still continue as per its nature, irrespective of whether one person or the entire worldly folk refused to accept it. These fundamental laws are not dependant on any mortal's acceptance for their existence. They are. They simply are. Period. In a similar vein, so is the law of karma. It exists, it simply exists. Period.

Whether you believe in 'you reap as you sow' or not, whether you believe in reincarnation or not, whether you believe in karmic debt or not, is irrelevant. Fact of the matter is that the law of karma is as irrefutably functioning in this world as is the law of gravity. Thus whether you believe in the concept of karma or not, the fact remains that it is affecting you right now and will continue to do so whether you like it or not, whether you accept it or not.

Now, if this is the irrefutable reality of your life, isn't it sensible to understand it, isn't it in your own interest to comprehend its working so that you can lead your life in an informed way? When you know that it is the bondage of karma that gives you pain and suffering, will you not want to break-free of this bondage? It is the law of karma that makes one experience the duality of happiness and sorrow. You have to put up with people you don't want to meet, and you cannot be with people you want to be with. The bondage of karma is very deep-rooted indeed. And somewhere or the other it was this fear lurking behind Arjuna's anguish – the fear of being pushed deeper into the bondage of karma by incurring sin from having to kill in the impending war of Mahabharata that laid the foundation for the Bhagavad Gita.

Yes, the apple will fall on your head and a returning boomerang will, but obviously, return. And remember, so will the consequences of your karma. Guiding the reader to understand its subtle nuances, accept and evolve from self-centred to selfless actions, emerge from the smothering smoke of ignorance, step down from the relentless wheel of karma and walk into the absolutely liberating freedom of being who you really are, is the plain, unpretentious objective of this book.

Chapter-1

VEDIC CLASSIFICATION OF KARMA

Most people would be familiar with the old, widely known adage: As you sow, so shall you reap. It entails that the seed which you sow will grow into a tree, and you will have to eat the fruits it ends up bearing. This allegory of seed and tree has great relevance in understanding the principle of *karma*. But the moot point is: What does *karma* really mean? In the Bhagavad Gita, Sri Krishna declares that it is indeed difficult to fathom the depths of the phenomenon called *karma*. Just as God is way beyond the remit of intellectual understanding, likewise it is extremely difficult to understand the working of *karma*. So what is *karma*?

Karma means action. Any action of the physical body induced by external or internal forces is known as *karma*. And the driving force behind the *karma* can be any desire, any emotion or any sensory impulse. Well, the impulse too can either be external in origin or may well be an internal one. For example, a wave of anger upsurges in your mind and you impetuously slap the other fellow. The discomposure, the excitement of the impulse of anger blinds your intellect such that heedlessly you end up performing a rash action viz. slapping or kicking someone. Likewise, many a time your actions are prompted by some desire or the other. Say you see someone driving his girlfriend on his motorcycle and this sight leads to a thought, 'I too want to take my girlfriend on a drive.' And thus motivated by that one desire, you seek your girlfriend out with the intention of fulfilling that desire. But say if you don't have a girlfriend, then you will burn in the fire of envy, cursing your fate that you don't have even a girlfriend! Thus the desire stops at the level of the mind for the body couldn't execute the action at the physical level. Nevertheless, the desire will reside in your mind and were you to get some such opportunity in the future, you will happily take some girl on a drive. If not today, then tomorrow!

Similarly, you see someone eating your favourite delicacy and the desire to eat that item arises in your mind – this is an example of external sensory impulse. You visit the sweetshop, buy the sweetmeat and eat it. The action undertaken by you, prompted by your desire, your emotion or by perception of an external impulse is *karma*. It can be exemplified through several daily life instances. You see someone getting married and this leads to a desire of finding a suitable bride or groom for yourself. You see someone having their lunch and a thought arises, 'I have to eat my lunch too.' You observe someone talking on the phone and this reminds you that you too need to call someone – these are all examples of external stimuli, impulses leading to physical actions. Thus, the changes occurring in your mind, via external or internal impulses, initiate some or the other action in your body. Such physical actions which are induced by internal or external stimuli or impulses, emotions or desires are called *karma*.

Now broadly speaking, *karma* can be categorised in various ways. One of the classifications is that of *viheet karma* and *nishiddha karma*. *Viheet karma* refers to *karma* which is sanctioned by the *Vedās* and scriptures, approved by our sages, and wise guardians of our society. Thus, all actions which ought to be performed as sanctioned, as authorised by Vedic, scriptural as well as religious and moral authorities are called *viheet karma*. *Nishiddha karma* is the polar opposite of *viheet karma*. Thus these actions are forbidden by our scriptures, *Vedās*, sages and the wise, for they are neither beneficial to the individual nor are they in the larger interest of society. There is a long list of both types. For example, the list of *nishiddha karma* includes lying, stealing, killing, envy and jealousy, mud-slinging to name but a few. Herein it is important to understand that such nefarious acts affect not only the other person but they also affect you. For example, every time you lie, your mind gets defiled; every time you steal, your mind gets sullied. Thus the bottom line is that one should be performing *viheet karma* and refrain from carrying out any *nishiddha karma*. This will be discussed in further detail later. Now, *viheet karma* is further sub-classified into four types:

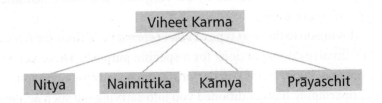

Nitya karma is neither good nor bad, for these actions give neither auspicious nor inauspicious results. And mind you, this is a type of *viheet karma* i.e. you ought to do them. So, what are these *nitya karmas* that bear neither *punya* nor *pāpa* but yet have to be performed nevertheless? Getting up early in the morning is *nitya karma*. So is carrying out spiritual practices in the morning and evening – in the transitional period between night and morning as well as between day and night. This transitional period is known as *sandhyākāl*. Thus doing *prānāyāma* and *mantra japa* at dawn and dusk i.e. *sandhyākāl* is indeed *nitya karma*.

At the level of physical body, taking a bath in the morning is an example of *nitya karma*. So are the acts of micturition and defecation. Paying respects to your parents in the morning is also deemed as *nitya karma* as is venerating your master, your elders and your teachers. All such actions bear neither auspicious nor inauspicious results. Now just because you don't do these things of your own accord, the sages had to give a dictum stating that by bathing early in the morning, by respecting your parents and elders, you earn *punya*. So that albeit for the carrot of merit, you will be tempted to carry out such *nitya karma!* Thus they had to link auspiciousness to such acts, but in reality such actions have nothing to do with *punya* or *pāpa*. By getting up early in the morning, breathing in the fresh air, bathing, you get refreshed, thus it is ultimately in your benefit. Likewise, you gain by carrying out spiritual practices at *sandhyākāl* – where is the question of incurring any merit or demerit. Thus in effect, *nitya karma* is neither good nor bad but is strongly advocated by our scriptures and thus constitutes a type of *viheet karma*.

Moving on to the next type of *viheet karma* i.e. *naimittika karma* – this involves doing actions for a specific purpose. These actions are not mandatory but if you perform them on specific occasions, if your upbringing has conditioned you into carrying out such actions, then it is a good thing. Now interestingly enough, not doing these actions amounts to doing *pāpa* but the converse is not true i.e. you don't earn any *punya* by performing them! Being charitable (giving handouts, donations) at the time of eclipse, full moon day or on some religious occasions or festivals like *Makar Sankranti, Guru Purnima* are some examples of *naimittika karma.* Our scriptures say so, and moreover they also state what should be donated and when. For example, on the occasion of *Makar Sankranti* one ought to hand-out jaggery and sesame seeds. Similarly, on the occasion of *Ganga-Dussehra*, it is said that one should offer milk to others.

Likewise, performing *shrāddha* (rituals performed as homage to dead parents, ancestors) is also a type of *naimittika karma*. Now whether this gives any *punya* to the departed souls is a debatable issue. But our scriptures do advocate doing so – they endorse being altruistic and donating generously in the memory of your departed loved ones. In effect, such scriptural dictums encourage otherwise greedy, covetous people to be charitable on at least some occasions; to loosen their purse strings at least sometimes! Although it is another matter that the *pundits* exploit these scriptural decrees to serve their own selfish purpose! 'Do donate, but give it to us', they declare to the gullible ones. My own personal view is that on such occasions be generous and part with some of your belongings but give to the needy – orphans, the destitute, those who are in desperate need of your aid. It is not at all necessary that you have to give only to a *pundit* or only to a *Brahmin*.

Shrāddha is anyway about paying respects to your ancestors – those very people who have passed on their wealth to you. Now even if you haven't inherited monetary or material wealth, you cannot deny the genetic inheritance, can you? So, donating money, reciting *mantras*, helping in the building of a hospital or a school and so on as homage to your dead parents or ancestors is an example of *naimittika karma*. Such actions are done for a purpose and our scriptures declare that not doing these incurs sin, but you don't gain any *punya* by doing them. For example, say a monk or a sage were to knock on your door and ask for something and in your arrogance you shoo him away – know that by doing so, you will incur sin. Likewise, say someone who is starving begs you for some food and you refuse – know that this rebuff on your part will certainly fetch you *pāpa*.

You have enough food but you refrain from satisfying the poor fellow's hunger – what kind of humanity is that? So that compassion, kindness, benevolence and generosity may thrive in society, our sages deemed even such acts of basic humaneness as *naimittika karma*. Thus if some such destitute were to seek your help, go ahead and do so wholeheartedly; if some sage, some monk happens to come to your home, you ought to serve him to the best of your capacity and ability. If you don't, then remember you will incur sin. But the converse is not true i.e. if you do show your charitable side, you don't gain any *punya*. Why, you may ask? Because that is your duty, where is the question of earning any *punya* in fulfilling your obligations.

Being a householder, you have a responsibility towards the society. Thus you ought to carry out all such benevolent actions. Feed the hungry, help the needy but don't expect any *punya* from doing so. Similarly, remember that on all the occasions when you could come to the aid of the needy but because of your arrogance or malevolence you don't, know that you will incur sin.

Moving on to the third type of *viheet karma* which is known as *kāmya karma* – these are actions carried out for the fulfilment of one or the other desire. In other words, desire-prompted actions are defined by our scriptures as *kāmya karma*. These entail all actions done for the fulfilment of any wish. And this includes *japa, mantra* chanting for some egocentric desire fulfilment. Interestingly enough, there are such *mantras* in our scriptures, the appropriate chanting of which leads to fulfilment of specific desires. For example, there are specific *mantras* for those desirous of acquiring wealth or begetting children, and yes, even for harming your enemies!

King Dashratha had performed a specific *yagya* for the fulfilment of his desire for a son. Mythology states that by virtue of that *yagya* he became the father of four sons. Thus in ancient times, people would perform all kinds of wish-fulfilling *yagyas*. But mind you, these actions were sanctioned by the scriptures i.e. they constituted *viheet karma*. On the other hand, those who would perform *nishiddha karma* for fulfilment of their nefarious desires were deemed as *rakshasas*, demons.

Vedās quote all kinds of *mantras* whereby through the performance of *viheet karma* one can fulfil one's desires – be it yearning for wealth, for sons etc. It is no surprise then that there are many so-called *babajis* who have made a thriving business by exploiting your greed, your desire for materialistic gain. Thus they ask people to meet them in private for some specific *mantras* and have their wishes fulfilled – become rich, beget a son, win an election, or eradicate diseases...! So, any *yagya*, any *mantra* recitation done with the motive of fulfilling one's desires is called *kāmya karma*.

This leaves us with the final type of *viheet karma* viz. *prāyaschit karma*. *Prāyaschit* means contrition, penitence, the sentiment of remorse wherein one regrets carrying out an inappropriate action. And our scriptures clearly describe ways of repentance through performance of specific actions which are known as *prāyaschit karma*. Indeed our scriptures are the final word, the final authority for everything! The story of Somnath temple in Gujarat illustrates *prāyaschit karma* very well. It is said that in order to repent for his sin, Indra had invoked Lord Shiva by performing penance in this very temple. Likewise, it is said that after slaying Ravana, Lord Sri Rama had observed the principle of *prāyaschit karma*. All his misdeeds notwithstanding, Ravana was a great disciple of Lord Shiva and moreover was the son of a sage. Thus as penitence for his action of killing Ravana, Sri Rama performed a *yagya*, recited *mantras* and prayed in remorse that given the circumstances, he had no other choice but to kill Ravana; but at the end of the day, the fact remained that Sri Rama had slayed Ravana. Thus, despite the fact that given Ravana's misdemeanours and transgressions, there was no other option but to kill him and yet Sri Rama had performed penance for this – why? This was because had he not done so, he too would have in effect sown a seed of *karma*. Moreover, by doing so he demonstrated that albeit for valid reasons, yet killing another being was wrong.

Similarly, after winning the war of Mahabharata, along with his brothers and his wife, Yuddhistra had performed a *yagya* as a means of expressing his remorse for having killed thousands of people in the war. This was his *prāyaschit karma*, his penitence. Again, Yuddhistra was well justified in killing the nefarious Kauravas, an act which even Lord Sri Krishna had endorsed. Nevertheless, the authority of the scriptures holds its own place and thus no matter who you are, if you do something unethical then you have to perform penance as an expression of your repentance.

This then is the broad classification of *karma* wherein, as per our *Vedās*, actions are classified according to those that ought to be done and those that one ought to refrain from doing. And there are eighty thousand *mantras* that cover all these aspects. Now who will read, who will remember, who will understand eighty thousand *mantras* and then bring them to practise in one's daily life? A colossal, hugely daunting task! If Sri Rama had to do penitence, if Indra had to do penance for his wrongdoing, then what about us lesser mortals who commit countless inappropriate acts and moreover are not even aware of them?! What's more, we have no clue about what is *prāyaschit karma*, how is it to be done, thus people fall in the traps of *pundits*. A grave, solemn problem indeed! But no need to worry, for Lord Sri Krishna has saved us from all this palaver, from all this paraphernalia by offering us refuge through the Bhagavad Gita.

Chapter-2

KARMA: WHAT THE BHAGAVAD GITA SAYS

Vedic texts are the ancient scriptures that lay down a lucid yet precise classification of *karma*. Taking into account the intellectual as well as emotional quotient of the people living in those times, the *rishis*, the sages had categorised *karma* into *viheet, nishiddha, nitya, naimittika*, *kāmya* and *prāyaschit,* as delineated earlier. And the entire society at large would follow the dictum. But as times changed, a decline in the intellectual calibre of the civilisation became clearly apparent. Thus we should all be immensely grateful to Lord Sri Krishna who blessed the masses by simplifying the concept of *karma* through the most distinguished ballad, the Srīmad Bhagavad Gita.

In a nutshell, the Gita classifies *karma* under two broad categories namely, *sakāma karma* and *nishkāma karma. Sakāma karma* entails actions driven by some goal, some ulterior motive. On the contrary, there is no such ulterior motive in *nishkāma karma*. The concept of *nishkāma karma* can be understood through the nineteenth verse in the fourth chapter of the Gita:

yasya sarve samārambhāḥ kāma-saṅkalpa-varjitāḥ
jñānāgni-dagdha-karmāṇaṁ tamāhuḥ paṇḍitaṁ budhāḥ

The one whose all undertakings are devoid of desires, who has relinquished all desires and motivations, whose all actions have been burnt in the fire of *gyāna* (highest knowledge) – the wise refer to such a being as a *pundit*.

How very incredibly amazing! No desire, no ulterior motive, no driving force, no *sankalpa* behind the actions. In fact, no desire to undertake, to commence, to start any action at all – when such a person performs any action, that is known as *nishkāma karma*! And contrast this with people doing charity, building hospitals, schools and claiming their actions to be *nishkāma karma,* but is it really so? Are these self-proclaimed do-gooders doing it for no reason at all? Are they not seeking any desired result for their actions? Sure they do! The advertised inscriptions in the entrance foyer of such institutions clearly reveal their ulterior motives: 'Dedicated in the memory of my late father or my grandfather so and so...' On the face of it these commemorative memorials may seem quite innocuous but they clearly reflect the lurking head of a massive ego! Likewise there are some so-called social workers who arrange mass marriages in the name of charity. But here they are patting their own backs for doing *nishkāma karma* and receiving funds with the other hand at the same time. Can this be labelled as *nishkāma karma*?!

Lord Sri Krishna gives the perfect definition of *nishkāma karma* – the one whose mind is expunged of all desires, expectations, motives – in fact there is no thought planning at all, yet actions happen through him or her. Now this may seem quite paradoxical to you. After all, can any action occur without any preceding thought, any preparatory planning? It sure is extremely difficult to even conceive this notion. Perplexingly amazing! 'Mind empty of all desires, all *sankalpa*...' – when does the mind become completely devoid of desires, *sankalpa*? In the depths of meditation! When the mind is totally absorbed in a heightened meditative state – that is the moment when there is no wave of desire, no *sankalpa* arising in the mind. But can any person perform an action in such a deep state of being?! It is simply not possible. Thus, the million dollar question is: Through whom can *nishkāma karma* take place? Well, it can happen only through a person who is ego-less and experientially knows the real Self in all its radiant incandescence. The one who has attained self-realisation, who verily knows his Self distinct from the body-mind-intellect and whose mind is completely empty of desires and *sankalpa* – *nishkāma karma* can happen only through such a man of self-realisation, because there is no more any 'doer' of actions. As long as 'I' exist, so will desires. And inevitably these desires will lead to some action or the other. But all such desire-driven actions constitute *sakāma karma* and not *nishkāma karma*.

Sakāma karma is further classified into two subtypes: *kāmya karma* and *prāyaschit karma*. Actions motivated by the desire to become rich, become famous or to beget children are all examples of *sakāma karma*. What's more, performing *yagyas* or chanting *mantras* with the ulterior motive of pleasing the said deity so that your wishes may get fulfilled is also *sakāma karma*. And bear in mind, serving your Guru with the intention of pleasing is also *sakāma karma*. 'I want to serve Gurumaa so that a pleased master will shower her blessings upon me' – this too is *sakāma karma*!

Thus it is extraordinarily rare to come across someone who does *nishkāma karma*, in the true sense of the word. It is a very widely abused, misused, misinterpreted term, for people think that simply being charitable or serving others is *nishkāma karma*. Therefore, get this very clear that as long as the notion of 'I am' and 'I am the doer' exists in a person, *nishkāma karma* can never happen through such a one.

Chapter-3

THE BACKDROP
OF KARMA

Now let's move on to the workings of the principle of *karma*, the functioning of the law, the cycle of *karma*. But before we delve further into this, you first need to understand the concept of *samskārās*, which means impressions, imprints on your mind. Just as the imprints of your feet on wet cement leave a permanent mark, likewise know that there are innumerable imprints or *samskārās* in your mind. All that you perceive in this phenomenal world gets recorded in your mind. Whatever your eyes see, your ears listen, your tongue tastes, your nose smells, your skin feels – all this sensory interaction gets recorded in your mind. Say if I ask you to recollect what were you doing on the 1st of January 1976, what will your answer be? You will scoff at it saying that how on earth is it possible to remember events that took place such a long time ago. Although your conscious mind will make light of this question, yet know that under the state of hypnosis you will accurately chronicle all the events that took place on that day. Now how is this possible? Simply because your mind is the best possible recorder, best possible bookkeeper of all that happens in your life.

No hard disc of any camera, any video recorder can ever match the calibre of your mind. At best these gadgets can record information for several hours, but your mind is such a fascinating hard disc which has a limitless capacity to record and keep on recording, for its memory space never runs out. That is why under hypnosis people can recollect not only the events that took place in their childhood but also in their previous lives. This is the basis of past life regression therapy. All this recorded information is stored in your *chitta*, which is the storehouse of mind.

You see a beautiful girl and a thought arises in your mind, 'I too want to be beautiful'. You see a luxury liner and think, 'I too want to go on a cruise', so on and so forth. Thus imprints are left on your mind. All that you perceive and the thoughts thus evoked leave impressions on your mind, which are known as *samskārās*. Now the process of leaving a mark on your mind is a non-discriminatory one, which means the mind stores all that it perceives without labelling anything as good or bad, auspicious or inauspicious, meritorious or unmeritorious. In this context let me narrate an incident: Once a woman was gang-raped and given her severe mental trauma she was referred to a psychiatrist for counselling. The therapist put the woman under hypnosis and as she delved deeper into her own psyche an astonishing fact was revealed that sometime in the distant past, she had secretly harboured a desire for having sex with multiple men at the same time. Now which of her *samskārās* could have given rise to this particular desire?!

See, the conscious mind is not aware of the countless *samskārās,* for they reside in the deep recesses of the mind i.e. in the *chitta*. It is these *samskārās* that give rise to *vāsanās,* which can be described as the stench or fragrance of your bad or good *samskārās* respectively. You can see the waves on the surface of an ocean but not the deep oceanic force underlying them. *Vāsanās* is the storm, the force of desire which has not as yet manifested into perceptible desires. When an earthquake happens, all that is visible to you is the destruction on the surface. But you cannot see the cause of the destruction, which is the movement in the deep tectonic plates. These movements occur very slowly and manifest as an earthquake only when the crucial point is reached. Likewise, you are not aware of the *vāsanās* lurking in the deep recesses of your mind. But when *vāsanā* matures, it crystallises into a desire which is experienced in the conscious mind. And when a desire ripens, gets seasoned, it takes the form of *sankalpa*.

See, not every *vāsanā* will mature and hence not every *vāsanā* will transform into a conscious desire. For example, whilst turning the pages of a magazine, you see pictures of mansions owned by celebrities or rich tycoons and a thought arises in your mind, 'this looks grand, wouldn't it be lovely to live in a house like this?' This way an impression is made in your mind. But you don't dwell on the thought because somewhere inside you know that you simply cannot afford it. Hence the *vāsanā* does not mature, does not consolidate into a desire. In contrast to desires, there is no possibility of actuation in *vāsanās*. But if you keep on brooding over it, then it transforms into a desire. Now compared to *vāsanā*, desire makes a gross presence in the mind. And this crystallised desire persistently runs in the background of your mind. There is no limit to the types of desires one may harbour – be it a desire to inherit the legacy of any business tycoon, or the desire to marry a Miss Universe, or to own a Ferrari...!

And when you keep on cogitating over any particular desire, again and again, then that takes on the form of *sankalpa*. This means making a firm resolve in achieving something that your mind is focussed upon. 'I have to do this. I have to obtain this by hook or by crook' – when a desire takes on the form of such a solid determination then it is inevitable that the resolve will translate into an action, *karma*. *Sankalpa* is the point of no return – it will transform into some action or the other. Thus the hierarchical relationship is as follows:

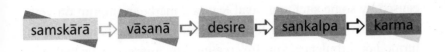

samskārā ⇨ vāsanā ⇨ desire ⇨ sankalpa ⇨ karma

Given all the sensory titillations in this materialistic world, it is no surprise that there is a constant onslaught on your mind leading to a storm of desires. There are scores and scores of desires in your mind but not every desire translates into a *sankalpa*. And know that if there are millions of desires in your conscious mind then there are trillions of imperceptible *vāsanās* and what's more, there are zillions of even subtler *samskārās* lurking behind the trillions of *vāsanās! Samskārās* are those seeds which have not yet sprouted. And when this seed of *samskārā* germinates, it leads to the sapling of *vāsanā* and then this sapling matures into a fully grown tree of desire with the branches of *sankalpa* finally bearing the fruit of *karma*. Thus there are countless *samskārās* and countless *vāsanās*. But not every *vāsanā* will crystallise into a desire. Moreover, not every desire can be fulfilled, can it? A woman met her friend after a long time and catching up with her she asked, 'I heard you got married. How is your husband?' The lady sighed, 'Well, I was hoping to marry a tall, handsome, intelligent man but how can you fight your fate, so I am coping with whatever I have landed up with...'

Thus people learn to compromise. They think they have obliterated their desires but the fact is that desire is a force and force can never be destroyed. Now the question arises: Why are *samskārās* formed in the mind to begin with, why are these imprints made in the first place? See, these deep impressions lying in the sub-conscious mind are caused by emotional turbulences and sensory experiences – be it pain, lust, greed, sensory or sexual indulgence etc. Now what causes turbulence in your mind? It is either due to uprising of anger, lust, greed, conceit, envy – the disturbance caused by some such upheaval leaves a mark, an imprint on your mind. Thus get this clear that whenever your mind is in a state of turmoil or turbulence, you are creating new impressions which will give rise to more *vāsanās,* a greater number of desires, innumerable *sankalpa,* which further entail a greater number of actions – a vicious loop indeed!

There is no dearth of sensory input, is there?! What all do you see with your eyes, what all do you listen with your ears and these sensory perceptions bring about some change, some disturbance in your mind – be it emotional change or disturbance at the level of thinking. When you think, 'this is so beautiful', it leaves a mark on your mind; 'how very gruesome, how awful' – it makes an imprint on your mind. Now look at your own selves. How many times a day do you make such exclamations, how frequently do such upheavals occur in your mind? Feeling good about something, feeling awful because of something, feeling excited by something and so on.

Once two *sādhaks* (spiritual seekers, practitioners) were travelling by air – one was a neophyte whereas the other was comparatively a mature practitioner. They were sitting in the front row, with a large viewing screen in front of them. A movie was being shown and it so happened that the frame moved onto an intimate scene of love-making. The amateur aspirant promptly shut his eyes and looked the other way. The other seeker continued to look ahead and seeing his companion's reaction, he questioned, 'Why did you shut your eyes?' The neophyte answered, 'Well that was a dirty scene and I didn't want my mind to get polluted by watching it.' 'But why did you continue watching?', he put a counter question to the senior seeker. The mature practitioner replied, 'To me they are just two forms, union of two shapes and no more than that. So, why would that scene create any turbulence in my mind? Hence, I did not perceive any need to close my eyes.' Now your situation is more like the neophyte seeker, isn't it?! Moreover, interestingly enough, what would the novice seeker have done in case he was alone and didn't have a fellow seeker sitting beside him? Would he still have looked the other way?! The son covertly watches pornography on the internet, hiding the act from his father and what's more, so does the father! Why? This is because sensual titillation is very enjoyable to the mind. And the mind is forever looking for joy – hence it takes it from wherever it can get it. The mind does not discriminate between the sources of the pleasure. It does not differentiate between joy obtained from the materialistic world and that from the spiritual realm. Thus know that sensual excitement, titillation gives rise to emotional turbulence and this in turn creates *samskārās*. This triggers the chain reaction:

samskārās → vāsanās → desires → sankalpa → karma

This is a continual process happening in your lives. In order to fulfil your desires, you get involved in strategic planning, brooding over it, repeatedly thinking about the desire, which eventually transforms into a determined resolve (*sankalpa*). And you start imagining how you would feel when your desire would get fulfilled, 'when I win the lottery I will do this, I will get that', 'when I own a Ferrari, I will drive to that place and then the other one...', and the more one day-dreams, the more is the likelihood of the desire taking on the form of a *sankalpa* which perturbs your mind, disturbs it such that it has no peace until the said desire gets fulfilled. Thus, every time your mind becomes restless, know that it is so because there is some desire or the other which is not getting fulfilled. Many people complain that their minds are not at peace and want to know the reason behind this. Well, the reason is your own unfulfilled desires!

This then is the backdrop, the science and the mechanics behind occurrence of any *karma*. In the subsequent three chapters, we shall delve deeper into the concept of *sakāma karma* and *nishkāma karma* as elaborately articulated by Sri Krishna in the Bhagavad Gita. Additionally, we shall understand the compellingly significant relation between your *prakriti* and *karma*.

Chapter-4

SAKĀMA KARMA

Sakāma karma refers to an action done for the fulfilment of a desire. Any action motivated by a selfish, self-centred, egocentric desire is known as *sakāma karma*. Now, the million dollar question is: Can you perform actions without any underlying desire? Fact is that all your actions, even a seemingly innocuous act of offering a glass of water to someone, are motivated by a desire lurking in your sub-conscious mind – the desire that the act be reciprocated when you are in need of it. Apparently, conscious mind may think that the action is selfless, a gesture of benevolence but in the deep layers of your sub-conscious mind lurks the selfish desire that has motivated the action. What's more, even with your Guru, you have the expectation of being rewarded in some way or the other. If nothing else, you expect the Guru to at least acknowledge your effort. My dears, if you do anything for the Guru, who is benefitting from that act, you or the Guru?! The fact of the matter is that when you offer something to the Guru, when you serve the Guru in any way, it is you who experiences a liberating feeling of love and gratitude. Why expect anything more, why expect any appreciation from the master then?

Now, many will deny harbouring any such expectation, but know that you will not find these desires and expectations in your conscious mind. Instead, if you delve deeper with increased awareness you will see all such cravings lurking in the deeper, sub-conscious and unconscious layers of your mind. The master is well aware of your maladies and that is why every now and then he offers some form of encouragement, so that you don't get dejected, you don't waver, and keep up with your practices enthusiastically. This perpetual need for appreciation even from the master is indeed childish and reflects a complete lack of surrender. Instead your attitude should be that every time you get an opportunity to serve, to donate, or to go on pilgrimage, you should be filled with utmost gratitude to the almighty Lord for all those chances. For what can you do if you don't get such invaluable opportunities?

There are scores and scores of people in this world who will never get any opportunity of even listening to these priceless words of wisdom. All they will do in their lifetimes is eat, sleep, procreate, get old and/or sick and then die one day. A life without devotion, without any service to the Guru, without any contemplation upon the divine – how can such a life be any better than that of an animal? Hence be grateful to the Lord, to the Guru and even to *Prakriti* that you are here listening to this higher knowledge. If *Prakriti* hadn't been favourable, your body could have fallen sick or any of your family members could have fallen ill and then instead of coming here you would have been paying visits to the doctor. Hence, make the most of all such opportunities.

In the Bhagavad Gita, the Lord says that the one who performs *sakāma karma* is only interested in those actions which are rewarding or beneficial. Such a person is interested only in gaining something. He won't do anything in which there is no profit or gain for him. Hence, people with such an attitude conveniently find certain tenets mentioned in the *Vedās* very appealing. For these state that if one performs certain activities like fasting, doing charity etc., then these actions will bear the fruit of wealth, good health, power, attaining heaven after death, so on and so forth.

'If you hold a fast on this day, you will get this; if you worship Lord Vishnu on this day you will gain prosperity beyond your dreams, for if Lord Vishnu is pleased so will be his consort Laxmi, the goddess of wealth!' And people with an endless list of desires in their mind happily follow all these do's and don'ts. They readily pay the priest a hefty amount to perform the *puja* in their homes. After all, isn't it easy to pay the priest who organises the worship (*puja*) in the comfort of your home and that too at such a breakneck speed! You think it is all worth it, because if just by doing this one can get access to all worldly riches, why bother then with developing the difficult virtues of honesty, purity, non-violence, equanimity of the mind, tolerance, dispassion and wisdom – such a tedious and arduous task! And who is desirous of attaining liberation from all bondages anyway?! It is only a rare being who seriously seeks absolute liberation. So why will he waste precious time in playing such silly games of organising *puja* through a priest?!

Those who perform actions with a desire to attain a certain result, their intellect is no more mature than that of a child who has to be constantly reminded by his mother about the fruits of his actions and only then will he do as he is told, for example, 'drink this milk so that you become strong and rank first in your class.' As soon as the child hears the words 'first in the class', he gulps down the milk knowing that it will lead to the desired result.

This world abounds largely with materialists and hedonists perpetually seeking sensory gratification. And such folk perform all actions with a desired result in their mind. They always ask 'what will I gain from this' before doing any action. And such people are happy to perform all kinds of rituals, observe all kinds of fasts etc. once they are told that these actions would bring wealth, good health, fame, eradication of miseries etc.

Let me elaborate this further for your understanding. It is said that fasting on a full moon day is especially rewarding, hence many observe fast on this day. However, not many know the true benefits of a full moon day or night. On the day of full moon, a beneficial planetary arrangement occurs and nectar is exuded from the lustrous full moon. But not everyone has the capability of drinking, absorbing this nectar. This can be partaken only by the one who knows the science of *swara yoga*, who has mastered *prānāyama*, whose mind is stilled. When such an individual performs certain specific *yogic* practices whilst gazing single-pointedly and unblinkingly at the full moon (*trātak*), he or she can absorb the exuding nectar which will not only impart good physical health but more importantly have a hugely favourable impact on his mind. Even if you don't know the specific *yogic* practices but can perform *trātak* on the full moon for a couple of hours, after having had only a light meal in the day time, it will impart a deep quietude to your mind.

Moon light has a great positive effect on the entire plant kingdom and hence vegetation flourishes during the night time. Thus, if moon light can affect the entire vegetation, can affect the sea tides, won't it affect your mind? It does have a very deep effect on your mind. Hence, if someone observes a fast on a full moon day with this understanding, then certainly it will be beneficial for him or her. But if someone blindly observes a fast on a full moon day with the desire of attaining worldly pleasures, then that becomes *sakāma karma*. So, fasting on full moon day can be done for attaining worldly pleasures which makes the act *sakāma karma*, whereas it becomes *nishkāma karma* for the seeker who observes the fast and performs his practices without any desire for worldly gratification.

When a priest tells one driven by worldly desires that some

bad omen will befall him, the fearful man requests the priest to do whichever ritual is necessary to save him from the predicament. He is happy to pay the priest to do whatever he thinks is appropriate. And this is how the priests are thriving in this money spinning racket. They exploit people's weaknesses. They realise that people are ready to do all sorts of things to fulfil their desires. Moreover, when they see that people are so lazy that they would rather pay the priests to get the rituals done, the priests make a lucrative business out of such folks' greed and lethargy. Hence first the priest will instil a sense of fear in the person by saying that you will lose your fame, you will incur loss of wealth, or a close one will harm you. And the daft fellow readily believes it all. When the priest sees that the 'victim' has been completely gripped by fear, he throws in a lifeline – do this *mantra*, do this *tantra*, perform these rituals, donate this and that – that's it, job done! And the foolish individual succumbs and does exactly as told, readily paying the priest a hefty amount without batting an eyelid!

In India, there are millions of people who perform such activities and think they are being religious, for they believe this is what religion is all about. And there is no dearth of priests, temples, ashrams who thrive on such business. Furthermore, they keep up with modern times – some have posh, air conditioned offices and smart receptionists who will sweet talk the clients and the foolish client will readily pay a huge sum to get his 'computerised' astrological chart which will be read by a so-called expert (read extort) astrologer! So happy are you to get fooled! A person desirous of specific results will readily perform all actions that he thinks are in his interest, even if they are lowly or underhanded. He is happy to follow ritualistic *Vedic* precepts which will give him worldly riches, but he has no interest whatsoever in the rest of the *Vedic* knowledge.

I remember, once I was travelling by air and there was this

co-passenger sitting next to me. Initially he was very happy and excited to see me and said, 'Ah ha! I am so fortunate to get *darshan* of such a renowned master.' Then sheepishly he asked, 'Do you only give discourses or do you also do any face reading or palm reading?' There was an emphatic 'no' on my part. But he persisted, 'any predictions, any *tantric* solutions to problems, anything at all?' Much to his chagrin, I politely replied that I don't do any of those things. On hearing this, his face fell dramatically just like a deflated balloon! It was indeed comical to see disappointment written large all over his face, on having to sit through the entire flight by my side, instead of the blonde bombshell on the seat behind!

See, people are not interested in masters for their higher wisdom. All they are interested is in their solutions to worldly problems. Hence, you will see huge crowds thronging the ashrams of so-called Gurus who allegedly promise to fulfil worldly desires. Get it clear that those who are ready to perform all sorts of acts for sensual gratification, for obtaining all kinds of riches, are doing *sakāma karma*. These people, who lack wisdom, are only interested in getting pleasure – be it from this world or other worlds (like heaven). For it is the lack of wisdom that makes these people seek ways of attaining materialistic pleasures even from hallowed texts like the *Vedās*, and that is all they are interested in getting from these esteemed scriptures. Such result-orientated folk are hoodwinked by fraudsters who prey upon their desire for materialistic gains. Those who are so attached to material prosperity and sense enjoyment, their intellect can never have a resolute conviction in wisdom or devotion. Their intellect is constantly vacillating and driving them to blindly follow anything and anyone heedlessly.

I remember once I had the misfortune of being in the company of a self-proclaimed pseudo *baba*, when I noticed that all people gathered there were carrying a bottle each in their hands. My curiosity was soon satisfied when I saw that everyone was approaching the *baba* asking him to touch their bottle – the belief was that the couple would be blessed with a baby boy! So all these zany characters, having locked their intellect in a safe place and thrown the key away into the sea, were blindly following the ludicrous act – all for the fulfilment of their desire for a son! It is another matter that such was the effect of my strong condemnation and reproach for that practice, that since then, let alone an invitation, I have never had any form of communication from that *baba*! Conceiving a son by touching a bottle? What a hare-brained mumbo jumbo! It reflects a complete lack of any trace of wisdom. Hence Sri Krishna labels such result-oriented fools as dimwits who completely lack intellect.

Thus be very careful. Be aware that you don't perform virtuous deeds with the desire of gaining anything, including Guru's appreciation. For if you do this then know that it will become *sakāma karma*. And it is very important to understand that no matter how much *sakāma karma* you do, it will not augment your *sattvaguna*. Why, you may ask. Because whenever a desire gets fulfilled by doing *sakāma karma,* it leads to the birth of several more desires. On the contrary when you perform actions without any underlying desire, these actions will increase your *sattvaguna* and this in turn will make your mind calm and collected. And anything is possible in such a focussed, integrated mind – even *samādhi* and self-realisation. See, why does the Guru love you, for what purpose? For no reason at all! After all, a Guru who himself exemplifies *nishkāma karma*, he alone can teach you *nishkāma karma*. How can a *sakāmi* Guru teach you *nishkāma karma*?

Many years ago, I had enrolled for learning music from a music teacher. But in the first few days it became apparent that the teacher was more interested in getting some work done through my father than teaching music to me, despite taking the fees on the first day itself! Now, contrast this with another music teacher I know who teaches his students earnestly for 10 to 15 hours every day but doesn't take a single penny in return, for he knows that music cannot be ever valued with money. If this is the kind of commitment needed towards music, then that should give you an idea of what depth of dedication is needed for acquiring the supreme most knowledge.

The enlightened one is well aware of how invaluable this knowledge is, hence it is only out of sheer compassion that he helps people on to the path of knowledge, for no other reason. He has no desire to get anything out of his followers and disciples. That is why I say that you are indeed extremely fortunate if you get an opportunity to serve such a *nishkāmi* Guru. I knew a great sage who lived all his life on the banks of the river Ganga. Once a minister of animal welfare landed up (as ministers do!) and with assumed magnanimity offered to give the sage some cows and buffalos. When asked whether he would like to get the animals, the sage kept mum. On persistent questioning, he calmly looked at me and remarked, 'All I drink is half a glass of milk and I can manage with what I have, so what will I do with all the animals?' Now if such a desire-less sage were to ever accept something from anyone, can you imagine how fortunate that person would feel? Such great beings don't want anything from anyone. And remember, you cannot enter the realm of such *nishkāma karma* without first killing your ego.

How many so-called social workers do you think have destroyed their egos? On the contrary, it will be rare to find one without an inflated ego, who doesn't do social service just to get applauded and get his or her photo in the media! And even if they don't have a fascination to be photographed, their egos nevertheless are bloated. They are indeed far, far away from humility and modesty despite their facade of servility. Thus to reiterate, as far as the doers of *sakāma karma* are concerned, all their actions are motivated by greed, by the desire for attaining something or the other, be it from this phenomenal world or from the celestial realms. Why others, look at your own selves. Do you remember doing any worthwhile deed without an underlying motive or desire?

Fact is that the desire comes first, action happens later! Even an innocuous act like scratching your head arises because of the desire to be freed from the uncomfortable sensation of itching. Without a desire, you won't even open your eyes in the morning. After all, why do people keep on sleeping until noon on a Sunday? Simply because there is no office, no school. Thus the question begs to be asked: Is it at all possible to perform actions without any motivating desire? Is this at all achievable? After all, can there be a tree without an underlying seed? Since action is that tree which emerges from the seed of desire, can the tree of karma be borne in the absence of the seed of selfish desire? Our revered sages, enlightened masters bear timeless testimony that yes, it certainly is possible to do so!

Chapter-5

NISHKĀMA KARMA

By now it must be well clear to you that as long as you are alive, you cannot stay without performing *karma*. But is it possible that although actions happen, yet there is no bondage of *karma*? Why look far – see the life of Sri Krishna himself. Did he stay engrossed in *samādhi* all his life? On the contrary, his life was full of diverse, colourful actions. He had to deal with one or the other troublemaker all through his entire life, right from his childhood – be it the demon Bakāsur, or his uncle Kansa, followed by a succession of enemies in his adulthood. There were occasions when he had to physically fight his enemies. And then, there were the times when he had fled the battlefield, and hence he was also known by the name 'Rancchoddās' – Sri Krishna could do that too! For if his wisdom guided him to flee the battlefield, then that is precisely what he did with no compunction whatsoever.

It doesn't matter what Sri Krishna did or didn't do, because for him *karma* was just a make-believe game. It is a fact that all actions performed after attaining the discerning knowledge of what the truth is and what the untruth is, are no more than part of a mirthful play. That is why Sri Krishna's physical presence on this earth is referred to as his *leelā*, which means divine play. What merit or demerit, heaven or hell, bondage or liberation, ignorance or knowledge! For Sri Krishna everything was just a play, be it frolicking with the *gopis* or romancing Rādhā or marrying Rukmini, relating the Gītā to Arjuna, or getting his entire clan destroyed by instigating infighting amongst his descendants – it was all no more than a play to him.

Whatsoever he did, he did with love and wisdom, with no regrets. Sri Krishna was the embodiment of the supreme consciousness, flawlessly perfect and complete in the real sense of the word. And he performed all his life's actions with detachment, being firmly established in the absolute truth, securely rooted in the eternal, indestructible, omnipresent existence. Such an attitude towards actions, such *karma* performed without any underlying selfish desire, without any expectation of getting anything in return is known as *nishkāma karma*. Such a person has no desires left, none whatsoever – not even the desire for *yoga-kṣema,* meaning there is no desire even for safeguarding the attainment of that which is unattainable. Sri Krishna says that for such evolved beings, who have transcended all duality and are firmly established in their true nature, the Lord takes on the responsibility of their *yoga-kṣema*. They need not worry about anything.

You have the choice to perform actions. And how you perform those actions is also up to you. But, says the Lord, you cannot dictate the fruits of those actions – it is not in your hands. Hence don't perform actions for any desired result. Furthermore, the Lord adds that don't think on the lines of why should I perform any action if I am not going to receive the desired fruit of the action? This too is inappropriate. Just perform your duties without any expectation of appreciation and without any desire for the fruit – neither gross nor subtle. Simply forego attachment to the result of your actions. Don't think about whether an action will result in success or failure, for this too is an attachment to the action, the *karma*. Failure or success should not stop you from doing your duty, your *karma*. Do all actions without any analysis of its likely fruit. But the way things are with you, a very common grievance is, 'I did so much for the other person but what did I get in return?' Or, 'I will do such-and-such thing for you, provided you remember this and return the favour later!'

I will narrate a story that is often quoted in this context. Once a sage saw that a scorpion had fallen into a pool of water. The poor creature was writhing in pain and was desperately trying to get out of the water. The sage compassionately picked it out and was just about to place it on dry ground when the scorpion stung him. The resultant pain made the sage's hand quiver and the scorpion dropped from his hand, back into the water. Nevertheless, the sage calmly repeated the process to help the creature, but the scorpion stung him yet again. And this kept on happening with the sage's every attempt to help the scorpion. Meanwhile a well wisher passing by, who had seen the entire drama, remarked to the sage, 'Why are you bothering to help this creature when it is repeatedly biting the very hand that is helping it?' The sage responded, 'See my dear fellow, it is the scorpion's nature to sting and it is a sage's very nature to be compassionate. And if a scorpion cannot forego his nature, can a sage abandon his?'

This is a perfect example of *nishkāma karma*. And moreover, he is not reminding God to make a note of his good deed! Now contrast this behaviour with your own – you call upon the witness of God for even the smallest of your acts! Fact is that you like to brag about everything and anything that you do, and moreover you ensure that others don't ever forget what you did for them. You say, 'remember, I was there for you when everyone else had left your side.' Well, how can the poor chap ever forget when you keep reminding him hundreds of times every day! Drop this attitude, my dears. Feel compassionate towards those who are in pain, in trouble and help them in whichever way you can without thinking about what you will or won't get in return. Do the needful without any desire for the fruit. Once compassion becomes your very nature, it will flow even to your enemies. You will regard them just as the sage had viewed the scorpion. Compassion, empathy and love will become an effortless part of your disposition and their fragrance will fill the very space you tread.

Do virtuous deeds, as this will make your intellect pure, and the supremely blissful *satchidānanda* will be reflected in this refined intellect. You will overflow with such joyous contentment that you will spontaneously share it with one and all. Then you won't have any expectation whatsoever from anyone. You will share your bliss without any discrimination and without expecting anything in return.

So reverting to the question, is it possible to do *nishkāma karma* i.e. actions without any desire for the fruit? Or putting it another way – who, if anyone, has the potential of performing *nishkāma karma*? Yes, it is certainly possible but conditions apply! The one who understands the value of this life, the one who has transcended the body, mind, intellect and has known his real identity, the one who has comprehended the meaning and the very purpose of this life – he alone can enter the ambit of *nishkāma karma*. Another question that arises is, how should one perform actions so that one doesn't get bound by them? Well, perform your actions deftly with an equanimous intellect, for it is this balanced intellect which will liberate you from all bondages. Such an intellect, which is laced with *sattvaguna*, has a firm conviction in not seeking fruits of actions. What will this lead to? You will not be bound to your actions anymore. And let me re-iterate, all this talk of *nishkāma karma* – don't limit it only to your behaviour with the Guru. Rather, it is meant for all aspects of your life, encompassing all actions irrespective of where you perform them and who you interact with, be it your children or your relatives. Remember, they are related to your body but no one belongs to you. Hence, behave with them in the same way that you behave with your Guru, with the same sentiments that you have for your chosen deity. And experience joy in giving – don't seek joy from someone or something, instead seek joy within. When you do your actions without any underlying desire, then you are not bound to your actions and life becomes no more than a play.

That is why Sri Krishna's life is called as a *leelā*; divine, but nevertheless no more than a play. And what is the motive behind any play? Why does a child fly a kite, what will he gain from it? The fact is that there is no purpose, no greed underlying any play; there is no ulterior motive, no desire of attaining anything at all. A play is simply, a play! The language of gaining something is the language of greed and ambition. Sri Krishna says to Arjuna, 'Don't be ambitious, just do your duty, neither desiring victory nor being afraid of defeat. A war that happens on such grounds becomes no more than a play. Yes, arrows will pierce the soldiers' chests, cannons might blow their heads off, but will they die, does anyone ever die? Is there anything called death at all?'

Life cannot be a play for a person who believes in death. So many heroes and heroines die in films – do they really die? But such is the effect of dramatic story-telling that the audience weep and sob their hearts out when the hero dies in a film. The interesting bit is that everyone who is mourning the death of one's favourite hero knows when his next film is due to be released, but despite that they snivel, shedding buckets of tears! See how the intellect gets deluded. You actually pay for the cinema tickets to watch a movie which you very well know is just a make-believe story, still see how you get carried away, how you get so involved with it;

you laugh and cry with the make-believe characters. Is there really anyone in the screen on which the film is being projected? But you still get so scared watching horror scenes that you inadvertently hold on to the arm of the person sitting next to you. Moreover, would you ever watch a really scary film, say like 'The Exorcist' sitting alone in a theatre?

You get scared of the horror scenes, but what if the film projection suddenly fails – will there be anyone in the screen? The screen will be as empty as it always was. Whatever is projected on that screen carries no meaning, then be it victory or defeat, birth or death. And the one who regards his own life as being no more real than the film projected on a screen, only such a person can be in the sphere of *nishkāma karma*. Then nothing will matter anymore, irrespective of whether he gains something or loses anything, whether he is honoured or dishonoured – for at the end of the day, life is no more than a play for him. That is why Sri Krishna always had a non-serious attitude. Here Arjuna is crying his heart out but the Lord is still smiling! For it is no more than a play for him. One who performs all his duties and actions with such an equanimous intellect, regards all happenings as merely being part of a make-believe drama. Then despite doing everything, such a one will not be tied down to his actions. Can the law of any land in this phenomenal world ever punish you for the murder you committed in your dreams? Hence the take-home message regarding *nishkāma karma* is that it can be done only by the person who sees everything as untrue, being no more real than a dream.

The Lord says that despite possessing all knowledge of this material world, if your intellect is not in equipoise then you will still remain in the bondage of *karma*. If you want to be freed from the bondage of *karma*, if you want to be liberated from the cycle of birth and death, if you want to transcend all miseries and drink the nectar of bliss, the only way is by doing all actions with an equanimous intellect. Now, this is not possible as long as you identify with your body. For how can anyone be freed of desires as long as he remains identified with his body and mind? As long as one regards the mind as 'I', how will such a person not regard every wave of desire that arises in the mind, as a desire arising within 'me'? And as far as the mind is concerned, it seeks supreme, everlasting, uninterrupted bliss. So until the mind attains the supreme bliss, how can it ever become empty of desires? That is simply not possible. Attaining supreme bliss is akin to attaining the supreme *Brahman*. This entails then that as long as you don't attain the supreme *Brahman*, your search for bliss will never be complete. And if you don't attain this bliss, the bubbles of desires will inevitably keep arising in your mind.

'I want pleasure', 'I want happiness', 'I want heaven' – all these wants are only as long as you don't know your real identity, your essential nature. But once you know, what can you then possibly long for? What can you possibly want? See, all divine incarnations have played a teasing game with their devotees. As long as the devotee keeps asking for something or the other, the Lord doesn't relent. But the moment he becomes desireless and enters the realm of *nishkāma karma,* the Lord says, 'ask whatever you want and I will give it to you,' and the devotee says, 'I don't want anything now' – such is the paradox! When one finally knows one's true Self, what can then one want from the untrue world? And only the one whose intellect is in equipoise has the capability of knowing that his real nature is ever-free, never in any bondage. On the contrary, the one whose intellect is agitated by waves of desires will not be able to digest and absorb this knowledge.

Know that if your intellect keeps getting stuck in the swamp of attachments, how will you be able to follow any path, be it *nishkāma karma* or path of knowledge or indeed any other path of liberation? So the first task is to get your mind out of the swamp it is stuck in. And this is possible only in the presence of *vairagya* (dispassion). So listen to what I am saying, says Sri Krishna to Arjuna, for only by listening will the fire of dispassion blaze in your heart and raze all your attachments. And the eradication of all attachments will purify your intellect. Your mind will become still and tranquil only when it gets firmly established in divine consciousness. Only then will your intellect be in equipoise with the consequential occurrence of *nishkāma karma*.

Now that is the pre-requisite for being able to do *nishkāma karma*. But look at all social workers who keep harping that they do *nishkāma karma* – it is not possible until and unless intellect doesn't get firmly established in truth, in the true essence of God. It is indeed a fact that no one can stay without doing actions. For even if you relinquish everything and go to reside in any corner of the world, you will still have to eat, drink, sleep, won't you? You will have to do some actions to obtain the food and in that process you will have to interact with some people, even if you don't know them. And whilst interacting with all sorts of people with diverse nature and temperaments, if your intellect is not equanimous then it will keep on getting agitated. If someone verbally abuses you, you will get angry. If someone praises you, you will get elated. If someone offers you quick ways of becoming rich, your greed will push you further down. In essence, only the one whose intellect is equanimous can play this game of life shrewdly and astutely. Then no matter where this person stays or which corner of the world he is sent to, he will play the game of life with perfect astuteness and gumption. Such a person can never err, for he is always in the state of being a witness. Hence, such individuals are perfectly geared up to live in this world because they fearlessly perform all their actions without worrying about failure or success.

Samādhi attained whilst sitting down in *padmāsana* (lotus posture) is *jada-samādhi,* for the body is insentient and how long can one sit in that position anyway? Maybe for few days, months or even years, but what after that? He will have to get up sometime. And then he will have to perform at least some actions. This means that the duration of the *jada-samādhi* is very short, whereas the time of performing actions is longer. Hence, the superior most state is being in *samādhi* even while one performs *karma*. Furthermore, only such an individual can do *nishkāma karma*.

And here the Lord is giving an invaluable advice. He says, 'don't worry when faced with an agitated mind or an intellect clouded by doubts – remember the tortoise and just withdraw the limbs of your senses, mind and intellect inwards. It will still your intellect, which in turn will make its conviction stronger.' Hence what this means is that meditation is crucial to attain the highest knowledge. This is the only way your intellect will become equanimous and only then will you be able to do *nishkāma karma* and live beautifully in this very world. Then you don't need to spend your life far away in isolation in some cave. Even if such a person works and performs worldly actions all his life, even if he doesn't shut his eyes for a moment, his state of being remains the same viz. stilled, equanimous, and firmly established in the *Satchidānanda Brahman*.

It doesn't matter where a *gyāni* lives, be it in isolation or in the midst of this bustling world, it makes no difference to his state of being. And this is what the Lord is saying to Arjuna – be established in the truth and perform your duty as your actions will not bind you anymore. In a way, the Lord is saying that even if people die at your hands in the war, you will not incur any sin, for the *karma* happening will be *nishkāma karma*. Following this path of *nishkāma karma*, the mind can break free of all bondages of *karma*. When you do *nishkāma karma*, in a witness mode, then such actions are no less than a spiritual practice. On the contrary, when you are attached to your actions, then those very actions will become a cause of your bondage. It is not what you do, but how and why you are doing it, that is what matters. You cannot stay inactive even for a moment. You may say how that is possible, for we are sitting in front of you right now and not doing any activity. Apparently it may look as if you are not doing anything, but in reality you are. After all, aren't you listening, isn't your intellect trying to make sense of the heard words? When your intellect gets baffled, the question mark can be seen right on your faces, in the frown on your forehead. And when you do understand something, it is reflected in your smiles. So, is action occurring or not?!

When you get overwhelmed by some of my words and tears well up in your eyes – isn't that an action? And you are nodding in affirmation, isn't that an action?! You are breathing, your heart is beating, blood is circulating in your body, your eyelids are blinking, your gut is digesting the eaten food – there are so many activities that are happening which your conscious mind is completely unaware of. You cannot refrain from doing actions even for a single moment. You cannot renounce actions. And if you think about it – you would have never been born, had it not been for the (sexual) activity performed by your parents. So, when this body itself is born out of action, then how can any person even think that he or she can stay inactive? It is absolutely impractical. Because everyone needs something from the other. Even a disciple is dependent on the Guru, for he needs the Guru to dispel his ignorance and that is why he serves and respects the Guru. So, really speaking, a disciple's service to the Guru cannot be regarded as *nishkāma*, for it is motivated by an underlying desire for liberation.

Karma intended for the Lord and offered unto the Lord is *nishkāma karma*. A devotee performs all actions with the attitude that everything belongs to the Lord, nothing is mine. And remember, other than the path of *gyāna*, the only other path leading to self-realisation, to enlightenment is the path of *nishkāma karma yoga*.

Chapter-6

PRAKRITI AND KARMA

Prakriti is the creative force, the material substratum of this entire manifest world and it functions through the three *gunas* viz. *sattva* (purity), *rajas* (motion or activity) and *tamas* (inertia, darkness). Our body and mind are borne of *Prakriti*, and it is due to the effect of its *gunas* that activities are occurring in them. In fact, all actions are influenced by these very *gunas*. One acts as per one's *prakriti*, one's innate, instinctive nature. If *rajoguna* or *tamoguna* is predominant, then such a person will be unable to do *séwā* or *nishkāma karma*. Such individuals are restless, full of anger and cannot perform actions without attachment. On the other hand, the one with dominance of *sattvaguna* has the distinct possibility of moving on to *nishkāma karma*. He will gradually move from *sakāma* to *nishkāma karma*. Hence, you need to see what kind of *prakriti* you have. If there is a precedence of *tamoguna* – inertia, lethargy, anger, unawareness and sleepiness – you need to work on reducing this attribute. For were you say to such a lethargic person, 'get up early in the morning and carry out the spiritual practices', will he be able to do so? Likewise, the one with dominance of *rajoguna* is very restless, fidgety and vacillating. Such a person is quick in calculating what he will get out of doing anything. He is focussed on the result, on the fruit of the actions, and also calculates when he is likely to get it. Such people are long-term planners. And even if such a person goes to a Guru to learn meditation, the first thing he wants to know is when will he get *samādhi*?! Hasty, impatient, hurried and wanting everything to happen quickly. Let alone *samādhi,* such a person will find it very difficult to meditate, for there is a lack of concentration. And this is because he lacks patience, satisfaction and tolerance. It is like a pregnant woman impatiently asking about the delivery time of the baby, when she is only in the first or second month of the pregnancy. Just as a baby needs to be nurtured by the mother for 8 to 9 months in her womb, likewise when you meditate and pursue your spiritual practices, it is going to take time for the practices to fructify. And it doesn't matter if you take only one small step at a time, rather what is important is that the step must be pointing forward – ensure that you don't go four steps backward for every step you take ahead.

I remember a story wherein a disciple goes to his master one day and says, 'Master, I will be unable to come to you for a month.' Up until then, this disciple had been regularly and sincerely practising under the guidance of his master. When the master enquired about the reason, the disciple replied that it was because he was getting married. On hearing this, the master's facial expression changed to that of grave concern. The disciple sensed this and asked him what the matter was. The master said, 'nothing, it is all right, and my blessings are with you.' But the disciple persisted as he had discerned that something was amiss. The master then revealed, 'this is not the first time you are getting married.' The disciple was perplexed, for he knew it was his first marriage. The master continued, 'you were my disciple even in your previous birth and at that time too you had sought my blessings to get married. But after marriage, you got so involved in your householder's life, you got so entrenched in attachment to your wife and family, that you forgot me and gave up your spiritual practices completely. And it was only when you grew old that you wept in remorse, having not taken out any time for your spiritual evolvement. You died with a wish for another opportunity, which you got in this birth as you did become my disciple. But today, you have made the same announcement and hence my concern for your future.' On listening to this revelation, the disciple was mortified. He pledged that he wouldn't commit the same error. He said he would first focus on strengthening his spiritual foundation, stabilising his mind, get firmly established on the path and only then would he marry.

Now, let me clarify herein that I am not against marriage. I am not saying marriage is an obstacle to spiritual growth. But it is equally true that priorities change after marriage. Thus it is in your interest to get fully trained before you jump into this relationship. And ensure that you and maybe your partner too are in regular touch with your master. If you continue with your spiritual practices besides being in regular touch with your master, then there can be no better institution than marriage to help you evolve spiritually. This is because marriage and family life provide you with the opportunities to work on extricating yourself from the grip of lust, greed and attachments. It is not necessary that everyone should lead the life of a celibate, but you need the basic training before you can enter a householder's way of life. See, once you get the training to drive a car dexterously, then you can drive whichever vehicle you want.

Our *karma* are influenced by our *prakriti*. It doesn't matter what sort of thoughts reside in your mind, what makes the difference is your innate *prakriti*. No matter how many words of wisdom you listen to, but if your *prakriti* is predominantly *rājasic* or *tāmasic*, then the heard words will stay in your conscious mind only for a while and then will evaporate. You will not be able to retain wisdom, you will lose it. Instead, your interest will remain in sensory gratification, in playing political games. And mind you, politics is not limited only to politicians; in fact everyone plays political games in their lives. Isn't there politics involved between a husband and wife, between parents and children, and between relatives? No matter if you don't like some relative, but on the face you pretend to be so warm – isn't that politics? In the name of maintaining societal norms, you play games with one another. And this gives rise to a lot of aggression – you pretend to be welcoming but inside you are seething in anger and aversion.

The precedence of *sattvaguna* opens the door to the possibility of performing *karma* without any attachment or expectation. By performing virtuous, benevolent acts viz. doing *japa*, charity, fasting, going to temples – even if they are motivated by the desire for attaining worldly things, it is possible that a day will come when just going to a temple or doing *japa* becomes a source of joy. Then the person starts doing these acts not for the fulfilment of any desire, but because they become a source of contentment and joy. Thus, even though a person starts off by doing *sakāma karma,* by virtue of his *sattvaguna*, a day will come when he will enter the realm of *nishkāma karma* where all actions will be performed with complete non-attachment. Hence, keep on performing virtuous, benevolent actions and do your spiritual practices with alacrity, for this changes the constitution of your *prakriti*. And once this happens, the strength of your virtuous deeds will result in minimising the effects of your previous misdeeds.

If there is even one person in a family who performs *sāttvic karma*, then this has a significant influence on the rest of the family members. And sages encourage people to perform *sāttvic karma* by dangling the carrot of *punya* (merit). They extol the virtues of good deeds, like getting up early in the morning, doing one's spiritual practices, being charitable and kind, as they increase the accrued *punya*, for people need some such incentive to do virtuous deeds.

In the Gita, Sri Krishna says, 'He who is ignorant, who is guided by his ego, believes himself to be the doer of all actions. And if you are the doer, then remember that you will invariably have to bear the consequences. Then you cannot escape the consequences of those actions.' The Lord says, 'If you want neither to be the doer and nor the bearer, you need to have the resolve that you are neither the body, nor the mind, nor the intellect. You need to have the resolve that I am the unattached witness, the non-doer, the eternal *Ātman*. And established in this knowledge, perform all actions perfectly without expectations.

Change your way of thinking, work on transforming your intellect, for once your intellect gets transformed for the better, your *prakriti* (innate nature) will change. And once your *prakriti* changes, your *karma* will change and consequentially your entire life will get transformed. In essence, everyone is performing actions as per their *prakriti*. Your *prakriti* is defined by your *samskārās* (past deep impressions on the mind) and your *sanskārās* (environmental and social conditioning in the present life). Hence, in a way, no one is responsible for their actions. For how can any court punish someone for a crime if the person was unconscious at that time? That's the reason why a child is always given less severe punishment for his crimes because of his immaturity, and likewise if the perpetrator of a crime is deemed insane, his punishment is accordingly reduced and he is sent off to a mental asylum for treatment.

Thus, if you want to change your *karma*, then rather than trying to change the *karma* directly, strive to change the *samskārās* which are the root cause influencing all *karma*. Bear in mind that you cannot change *karma* just by changing your thoughts. There are many so-called intellectuals who have assimilated wide knowledge from diverse books, but nowhere can you see the implementation of this knowledge in their day-to-day life. What is the use of such bookish knowledge which doesn't bring about a transformation in your life? And this really puts Gurus in a very difficult situation, for however hard they may try, they cannot change the *prakriti* of the disciples. Hence, they have to keep on working on the disciple with great patience and perseverance. Having said that, remember that a Guru can only work on the one who is a disciple in the real sense of the word. And a disciple is a disciple only if he has genuinely surrendered to the master, else what can the Guru do?

Understand this process – *samskārās* influence *prakriti*, which in turn influences your thoughts and which finally translate into *karma*. So, if you really want to change your life then you will have to work on your *samskārās,* for when *samskārās* propel an upsurge of thoughts, it can shake the foundation of even the most grounded person. Beguiled by *prakriti*, ignorant beings get attached to their actions whereas the wise do not, for they are well versed with the working of *karma*.

Prakriti is very powerful, in some ways, more powerful than divinity. Although divinity resides within all, your behaviour is propelled by your *prakriti*. Such is the magnetic force of *prakriti* that you cannot see the divinity dwelling within you. And driven by the dominant *guna*, you get involved in such an intricate web of *karma* that even God dwelling within cannot do anything about it – such then is the power, the force of *prakriti*. *Prakriti*'s three *gunas* form this entire world, this entire creation. Hence, you cannot get rid of the influence that the three *gunas* have on your mind. You can certainly minimise their influence but cannot eliminate it completely. Even an enlightened being needs to sleep at some time or the other, and what is sleep other than an influence of *tamoguna*? When his body gets tired and he feels lethargic – even that is *tamoguna*. Likewise, he too has to eat when he gets hungry – digesting is all related to *rajoguna*. But there is a crucial difference. The *gunas* are in the control of the enlightened one, whereas the ignorant one has no control over the *gunas*. Thus, the seeker's task is indeed very daunting, for changing the innate nature of one's mind is a colossal challenge. It needs a great deal of courage but you can do it if you are willing to work hard, consistently and persistently.

To get unattached from the actions happening under the influence of *Prakriti* and its *gunas* is the biggest hurdle. And to achieve this requires a great deal of wisdom; one needs to be aware at all times. A seeker with *sāttvic* disposition and predominance will always eat sensibly, in limited quantity, for he knows what is beneficial for his health. Furthermore, he is aware that he cannot afford to waste precious energy in digesting food, as that energy is to be utilised for spiritual practices. On the contrary, a person with predominance of *rajoguna* has no control and will eat injudiciously. And let me tell you, the control and the discipline that you exert on yourself, of your own free accord, is what really works. If the Guru makes you do things against your wishes, you will rebel. Your mind will keep questioning why – why should I do this or that?

It is indeed difficult to be a disciple, for being a disciple means bringing death to your *tamas*, your ignorance. It is not easy to change one's mind, and it needs a great deal of courage to bring about this transformation. Just as the body's functioning is closely linked and influenced by your genetic code, likewise the functioning of your mind is linked to and propelled by your *prakriti*. It is your *prakriti* which influences your behaviour – what you think, how you speak, what you do, your opinions, and your entire personality. For example, a *rajoguni* person is always in hurry and does everything with haste – he gulps down his food, walks with a heavy stamping gait and speaks very loudly. On the other hand, a *sattvaguni* individual speaks in soft mellow tone and all his actions are measured, balanced and in moderation. Whereas a *tāmasic* person does everything very lethargically, whether it is eating, speaking, walking – he is full of inertia. Thus, as is your *prakriti*, so is your *karma*. Your *prakriti* has a very deep impact and influence on your emotions, thoughts and actions. So don't get perturbed by others' actions; out of ignorance, they are acting as per the influence of their *rajoguna* and *tamoguna*. When you know that the spouse is a personification of anger, why expect him or her to talk sweetly to you? Hence, whenever he or she throws a tantrum, just be cool. Understand that he or she is acting as per the influence of their *prakriti* and, in a way, are helplessly driven by it.

But how many people analyse their *prakriti*, their innate nature? How many people lead their lives without any self-assessment, reflection or contemplation on their behaviour, attitude and life? Such living is no better than that of an animal. The one who is tied down with the rope of his desires is no better than an animal. The one who is trapped in the bondage of his *samskārās* is, in effect, no better than an animal. These *samskārās* lie in the depth of your unconscious mind and you are not at all aware of them. Thus be very clear what the path of spirituality is – it is not about learning to be conscious, but rather the spiritual path is all about uncovering your unconsciousness with your consciousness. The day you become aware of all the seeds, the deep impressions, the *vāsanās* lying in your unconscious, that will be the day when you would start to live consciously.

Chapter-7

CONSEQUENCES OF KARMA (PART-I)

There are two types of consequences, two types of fruits of any *karma* – visible and invisible. Visible consequence is that part which is obtained immediately as a perceptible result, for example when you steal from someone, you experience fear of getting caught, your heart starts racing. On the contrary, when you serve others, especially your master, you experience peace whilst doing so. These are the immediate consequences of your actions. As in the case when you lie, when you steal, when you do something inappropriate, it leads to releasing stress hormone 'cortisol' in your body. And chronic stress leads to heart diseases, hypertension and even mental disorders. That is why, when a seasoned liar argues that there is nothing to lose by lying, he needs to understand that the body and the mind have to pay the price. Similarly, when someone steals, he perpetually lives in the fear of getting caught. Moreover, when he does get apprehended, the disrepute gives a greater degree of pain and distress.

Say if I ask you to recollect some incidents from your childhood, it is more than likely that you will easily remember occasions where the teacher had humiliated you or punished you in front of your classmates. Someone will recollect his father or mother beating him up. All such incidents where you had perceived physical or mental pain and distress are easily recollected because the mind holds on to such unpleasant experiences very dearly. Now why is this so? This is because when someone is being humiliated or abused, at that moment the person's attentiveness is very high, for he knows that everyone is watching. This increases the level of pain he perceives manifold, whereas the level of distress is much lower if no one is watching. Say a child falls down whilst walking on a road but there is no onlooker, in such a case the child would get up himself and start walking. But if the same child were to fall at home, the child wails his heart out for there is the mother rushing to his side, the grandmother fussing all over him – this attention that one gets from others enhances the perception of pain or pleasure. That is why it feels so good to receive a prize or a trophy in front of so many people. It is not the trophy itself that makes you happy but rather it is the laudation that one gets from so many people felicitating you – that imparts a feeling of great joy. Thus you never forget incidents where you got lots of attention from people, be it winning a school sack race, securing first rank, or being thrashed up in front of your mates or siblings. It is this attentiveness quotient that imparts a visible, perceptible consequence in that very moment – be it pain or pleasure.

The invisible result is the seed sown in your mind in the form of *samskārā*. For example, say when a child is being thrashed by his teacher, he will endure the beating but the experience might leave an imprint on his mind – a thought will arise in his mind, 'Thrash me now but I will settle the score some other time for sure.' That is why almost every person remembers some such school teacher who insulted him or beat him up. Just as this experience of pain sows a seed of future *karma*, so does the experience of pleasure.

Say, you are sitting by your master listening to the profound words of wisdom and your mind experiences a great deal of peace and joy – this is the immediate visible result of the *karma*. The invisible consequence is the purification of your mind, and furthermore the seed of desire it sows viz. wanting to be with the master again. Thus *samskārā-vāsanā*-desire form the backdrop of *karma* but then the *karma* sows the seed of another loop of *samskārā-vāsanā*-desire. Thus the loop goes on and on.

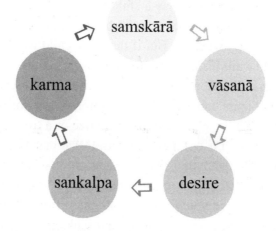

Let's take a look at the mind where all of this actually happens. What is it that goes on in there? If you observe meticulously you will find that the mind keeps mulling over objects again and again. And then it fantasises, imagines the excitement it would feel upon attainment of the said object. Thus it keeps on day-dreaming, vividly imagining how wonderful it would be when the desires would get fulfilled – how lovely it would be when I get married, how happy I will be when I get my degree, how ecstatic I will be when I will have my first child, so on and so forth. Thinking, brooding, fantasising and visualising the desire fulfilment – mind is the best cinematographer and the best screen play writer! It spins such enjoyable stories and derives so much pleasure from them that it continues thinking and day-dreaming about something or the other. And once the thinking is done with, it then moves on to strategically planning as to how soon it can attain the desired object or objective. It is the execution of this shrewd planning which is called action or *karma*. In this context, let's understand verse sixty-two from the second chapter of the Gita:

dhyāyato viṣayān puṃsaḥ saṅgas teṣūpajāyate
saṅgāt sañjāyate kāmaḥ kāmāt krodho 'bhijāyate

Your mind keeps contemplating upon the objects of sensory gratification. And this obsessive pre-occupation, repeated mulling over the sensory objects, leads to the development of attachment for the said objects. And from attachment arises the desire for attainment. But if this desire is not fulfilled, it leads to rising of anger in the mind.

See, when the mind is full of desires, it loses the ability of logical reasoning, rational thinking. For when an impure mind is consumed by any desire, it will want to achieve it by hook or by crook. That is why I see many people who although show a very servile attitude in front of me, nevertheless I am well aware of their misdeeds done as a result of their desire-laden impure mind. And when desires are not fulfilled, the frustrated mind is consumed by anger which impedes rational thinking. This sequence is beautifully illustrated by Sri Krishna in verse sixty-three of the second chapter:

krodhād bhavati sammohaḥ sammohāt smṛti-vibhramaḥ
smṛti-bhraṃśād buddhi-nāśo buddhi-nāśāt praṇaśyati

Anger leads to indiscretion as well as lack of discernment and judgment. From anger comes delusion, which leads to loss of memory, thus forgetting oneself and one's relationship with others, one loses all sense of proportion. From such loss of memory, arises destruction of the intellect (discriminating faculty) which inevitably leads to total downfall. After all, when the intellect is wrecked, what will be left then? When the mind is continually obsessing over objects, how can it ever be at peace? Thus a person consumed by desire to attain an object or objective will forever be frustrated, agitated. He will always be planning ways to attain the said object. And when he fails to do so, he will be swept off by anger, such that his power of discrimination and discernment, his intellect gets destroyed. Now what can one say about such a devastated being, says Sri Krishna. Thus you need to be vigilantly aware of all that is going on in your mind, for otherwise the consequences can be disastrous, to say the least.

Now let's look at some examples of fruits of *karma* (*karma-phala*). When you bathe, the immediate result is the feeling of freshness which you perceive instantly, and the latter consequence is that by keeping your body clean you avoid bodily infections. Moreover, people like being with you because there is a pleasant freshness in your personality. In a similar vein, what are deemed as *punya karma* are actions which make you feel good and at the same time impart joy to others too. Likewise, when a criminal commits a crime, others suffer but so does the perpetrator of the crime. He is filled with the fear of getting caught, and as alluded to earlier stress releases harmful chemicals in the body which lead to all sorts of diseases. Thus the consequences are borne by his body, and then he will also have to face the punishment meted by the law. Even if say, the criminal escapes the law, will he be exempt from any castigation? No! His own mind will punish him with the whip of fear, remorse and pangs of conscience!

The same goes for those who are easily consumed by anger. Stress hormones like cortisol and adrenaline will ensure that such people become prone to ailments like hypertension, peptic ulceration and heart diseases. Thus in a nutshell, our actions have an effect not only on others but also on our body and mind. A kind gesture, labelled as *punya karma* by our scriptures, fills the heart with warmth, joy and love. Thus it benefits others and is favourable for us too. On the contrary, inflicting pain and harm upon others, labelled as *pāpa karma*, has an unfavourable effect on our own mind and body; it makes one hardened, cruel and animalistic. So, be it bathing in the Ganga or sitting beside a sage or feeding the hungry or helping out the needy – these are all categorised as *punya karma*. But the important point is that all these actions have an inherent 'feel good' factor and thus you immediately perceive a sense of joy, warmth and satisfaction, which in itself is the delightful consequence of such noble actions.

See, the fact that you are all sitting here and listening to me – this too is a *karma*. It denotes that a *vāsanā*, a desire to be with the master, listen to the words of wisdom, must have been there somewhere in your mind. Thus you must have started planning and then managed to come here. Now what is the consequence of your action? Whether you will get any *punya* by coming to the ashram or being with me, I don't know about that! Although the scriptures say, it does. In fact, especially in context of olden times when transport was grossly underdeveloped, scriptures say that the *punya* accrued by visiting and bathing in the *triveni* (the confluence of three rivers in Allahabad) ten times was equivalent to that attained by a single offering of water to a sage for bathing! But isn't your mind experiencing warmth, calm, joy or contentment now? This is the visible consequence of your action. So who cares whether there is any *punya* or not, isn't the immediate, visible result enough motivation to do so?

Chapter-8

CONSEQUENCES OF KARMA (PART-II)

Before delving further into the results of past, present and future *karma*, let's look at some specific categories of *karma* from this context:

෬ *Sanchit karma* is the accumulated stockpile of *karma* i.e. sum total accrued over all previous lifetimes.

෬ *Prārabdha* is that part of your *sanchit karma*, the fruit of which you receive in your current lifetime.

෬ *Kriyāmān karma* refers to actions happening in the present moment.

෬ *Agāmi karma* refers to two things: Firstly it points to the fruits of your present actions which you will receive in the future, and secondly it refers to the future *karma*, the cycle of *karma* (as explained in the earlier chapter) due to the force of your previous and current *samskārās* and *vāsanās*.

Sanchit karma can be understood as your total bank balance, all your savings to date. This has two broad sub-accounts – one is where all your *punya karma*, (virtue or merits) get deposited and the other accumulates your *pāpa karma* (sins or demerits). Now just as every saving account generates some interest, which can be taken monthly or annually, know that whatever fruits you receive in your present moment, from either of the sub-accounts, are known as *kriyāmān karma*. Thus, your *sanchit karma* influences your present moment and simultaneously you keep receiving the fruits of your accumulated (*sanchit*) *pāpa* and *punya*. As I have already related, you will have to reap whatever you have sown, one day or the other, for every action generates an equal reaction. Thus all seeds sown in the bank account of your *sanchit karma* will inevitably fructify i.e. you will most certainly have to bear their fruits. So, know that all that is happening in your life right now, in your present moment, is a consequence of your own past *karma*. At the same time, your current actions will influence and shape up your future. And mind you, there are no exceptions herein – thus all your present actions will invariably have a bearing upon your future.

Now use your imagination and try to visualise a scene wherein there is a horse-rider in an open field with a cow standing some yards ahead and there are some deer much farther away. The rider is an archer and thus has a quiver (arrow-holder) on his back, holding a set of arrows that were shot in the past. One arrow is on his bowstring which is yet to be released, but the archer has just shot another arrow which although intended for a deer, has hit the cow. This is a vivid description and hopefully you can imagine it clearly. Now, using this graphic image we will draw a parallel with the above mentioned types of *karma*: The archer wanted to kill a deer but instead, unwittingly, he killed a cow. Hindus regard the cow as holy and sacred. It is said that whole pantheon of 33 crore deities reside in a cow. Many people take this literally but know that it is a rather poetic symbolisation created by our *rishis* to illustrate how every aspect of the humble cow nourishes humans and furthermore even has medicinal properties. In this illustration, the archer had no intention of killing the cow, his target was a deer, but irrespective of his motive, the fact is that, albeit inadvertently, he killed a cow. No matter how much he regrets his action, there is no way he can undo it, for there is no way the arrow piercing the cow's body can be made to revert back to the quiver. The action cannot be undone, and thus the archer will have to face the consequences, both visible as well as invisible results, of this *karma*.

So, the arrow which had already been released from the bowstring and hit the cow cannot be retrieved. But the archer can use his intellect and decide not to release the other arrow, which is yet on the bowstring. It is another matter though to figure out what are the realistic chances of the archer not shooting the second arrow? After all, his desire of killing a deer has still not been fulfilled, so it is more than likely that he will not go back until his aim is accomplished. Nevertheless, you may have deciphered by now that in this allegory, the quiver with the collection of previously shot arrows is a metaphor for *sanchit karma*. Whereas, the arrow that has hit the cow, that action is *kriyāmān karma* (action happening in the present moment) and the arrow on the bowstring is *agāmi karma*, in case the archer decides to shoot another arrow. But say hypothetically, the archer gets filled with intense remorse; he deeply regrets his act of killing the cow. And this contrition proves life changing, so much so that he breaks not only the arrow on his bowstring but all the remaining arrows in the quiver. This means that he will never release arrows in the future. And having emptied the quiver i.e. having exhausted the *sanchit karma*, the game of *sanchit* and *agāmi karma* comes to an end then, isn't it?

Just as time can be segregated into past, present and future, likewise is the game of *kriyāmān, sanchit* and *agāmi karma*. But whilst playing this game, you need to understand it clearly that the cause of your sorrows, your pain and suffering, is your own *sanchit karma*. And the part of the accumulated *sanchit karma*, the fruit of which you have to put up with in this lifetime is your *prārabdha*, based on which you receive happiness or sorrow, togetherness or estrangement, health or disease, poverty or abundance. But people find this very difficult to accept. That is why whenever anyone has to face loss or deal with disease, they curse the Lord saying, 'God gave me all these troubles!' But the law of *karma* is the veritable truth; it is an irrefutable fact which is accepted not only by *Sānkhya* philosophers and practitioners of *Ashtānga yoga* but also by Buddhists (who otherwise don't believe in *Ātman*) as well as the followers of Jainism who don't believe in any God as such – but all these schools of thought nevertheless veritably accept the principle of *karma*.

All these philosophies wholeheartedly accept that one has to reap what one has sown, and all sentient beings are inextricably linked with the law of *karma* such that there are no exceptions. As detailed earlier, even Rama had to do penitence for his *karma* of killing Ravana; a victorious Yuddhistra too had to do *prāyaschit karma*. What's more, at the end of the Mahabharata war, when Sri Krishna had gone to meet Gandhari to offer his condolence, an inconsolable and infuriated Gandhari had cursed Sri Krishna saying, 'Just as I have had to painfully witness the deaths of my children and grandchildren, O Krishna, I curse you that you will also have to mutely witness the annihilation of your clan.' The inimitable Lord Krishna happily accepted her malediction replying, 'Dear, thy wish will be granted. My descendants will all perish in front of my very eyes. But there will be one difference. Unlike you, I shall not grieve their deaths. Thus I wholeheartedly accept your curse and my progeny will die, but my self-illuminating knowledge will remain untouched because now nothing can ever make me sorrowful.' The one who has become choiceless, who does not discriminate between joy and sorrow, how can anything ever torment such a liberated being?

So, remember that just as previous *karma* are influencing

present moment, so will present *karma* bear an effect on the future. No one has ever been able to stop the fruit of *prārabdha,* nor will anyone ever be able to do so. That is why it is called *prārabdha,* pre-destined, for it is that arrow which has left the bow string, never to return. Such is this intricate loop of *karma* and its consequences. And it takes a braveheart to extricate oneself from the vice like grip of *samskārās → vāsanās → desires → sankalpa → karma → samskārās → vāsanās → desires → sankalpa → karma*

Chapter-9

IS THERE A LOOPHOLE
IN THE LOOP?

Now the million dollar question is – how to quit this game of *samskārās→vāsanās→desires→sankalpa→karma*? Is this at all possible? Yes, it is possible but only when you start having command on all the thoughts arising in your mind, on all the *vāsanās*, on all the *sankalpa* – now, how can this happen? By contemplating, meditating, experiencing, 'I am not the mind'. So, how does one experience the distance between 'I' and 'mind', you may ask? The tools are: de-attachment, dispassion and vigilant witnessing which will lead to calmness and awaken the power of discrimination (*viveka*). Then the present will be filled with supreme wisdom, putting an end to all *agāmi karma*.

See, why did *sanchit karma* happen; why and how did the *karma* get accumulated in the first place? This is because you see yourself as the mind, identify yourself with the mind, and because your mind is full of all kinds of worldly passions. You regard your body as your identity, your 'I', because of your ignorant mind. As a result of ignorance, people regard their disease-prone, decay-prone, ever-changing body as their 'I', their identity. Thus all relationships of the body are taken to be 'my' relationships by the ignorant ones; thus comes in the notion of 'my family', and the family's religion, caste and creed is taken on as 'my religion, my caste, my creed'. Essentially one regards that which one is not, as one's 'I'!

Now what does your ignorance-filled mind want, what does it yearn for? It seeks pleasure, joy, happiness! And the societal training is that one gets happiness from eating good food, wearing expensive clothes, indulging in sexual and sensual pleasures, drinking alcohol, hoarding latest gadgets, so on and so forth. Thus your mind has been trained to attain and derive joy from sensory objects. In effect you are brought up with the notion that only worldly objects and people can make you happy. Advertisers exploit this human weakness, hence blatantly splash all over the media that buying their brand of items, be it clothes, perfumes, jewellery etc., will make you complete.

And when a person repeatedly comes across this statement, he or she starts yearning for the said object, believing that it will make him or her complete. But the moot point is, why is the mind lusting after this objective world anyway, why is the mind inherently pursuing this world of things and beings? Essentially, the mind wants to know who or what it is; it wants to understand its origin, its roots; it wants to know what will make it complete, whole. But because of the inherent ignorance, the poor *Jiva* does not know where and how to look. Thus, hoodwinked by so-called relatives – parents claiming he is their son, siblings claiming he is their brother, grandparents claiming he is their grandson, the poor child starts believing them. Thus the child believes his existence is dependent on the parents and relatives. So he desperately seeks to be with them to feel safe and secure. Alas! The child ends up accepting the mother to be his mother – when she is not; the father to be his father – when he is not. What's more, the body that he calls 'I' is not his real identity either. Body is just like your garments –

by changing your clothes, you don't change, do you?

But having said this, I know that for you this is merely a statement because it is not yet your own experience. And as long as you don't see yourself to be separate from the body, there is no way you can ever know your identity distinct from your mind. People often ask, 'when will I attain self-realisation?' You can know your real Self only after you have first known your mind and clearly experienced your distinction from the body. Your problem is that you identify with the body and then ask, 'when will I attain self-realisation?' 'I am this body' – now tell me when will I become a man of realisation? Never! You see the external world through your eyes but can you see your eyes with your own eyes? Now some may argue that they can see their eyes in the mirror. But do you know that what you see in the mirror is a lateral inversion, a left-right reversal of the actual reflected object?!

But even if we accept the image seen in the mirror as a rough image of your eyes – say if there is no mirror, no pool of water, no reflecting surface, can you then see your own eyes? You simply cannot see your own eyes. Let's delve a bit more into this. Do your eyes see or is it your brain that sees through the medium of the eyes? See, when your eyes are focussed upon any object, a reversed (upside down) image is formed in the retina and the occipital cortex of the brain corrects this inverted image and visualises it correctly. But in essence, you don't see the external object but the image formed in the retina. It is the brain that makes sense of the image and hence you know it is a table or a chair and so on. Thus, that which your brain is unaware of, you will not see that object even if it is kept right in front of you. Fascinated by this fact, scientists are keenly investigating as to whether the world that we perceive is really as it is or are we seeing what our brain is projecting to us instead?

When Columbus was on his voyage of discovery, he happened

to land on a small remote island. Now it was only when the ships actually anchored near the island and the inhabitants saw people getting out of the ship, that they could identify it as a definite object. Until then, although the ships were close to the shore, all they could see was waves. They simply couldn't see the ships because their brain didn't know what a ship was! When faced with an object your brain has no knowledge about – you will be clueless, totally blank. Thus it is not your eyes that see, but rather it is your brain, your mind that sees through the medium of the eyes. The brain matches the images with the information stored in its memory neurons and then says this object is such and such. It is the mind that experiences the sensory world and then labels those objects, those events, those places as good or bad, pleasant or unpleasant and this information then gets stored in memory bank.

So in a way, whichever actions that have occurred through your body, be it *pāpa* or *punya*, the instrument behind the body that effected those actions is none other than your own mind. Thus technically speaking, all actions are in effect carried out by the mind and not by 'you'. But this is a mere hypothesis for you because you don't know who 'you' are, do you? You are in the waking state now. So if I were to ask you, 'who are you', it is more than likely that you will state your name, your profession, your relationship to some people etc. But in the realm of deep sleep, would you remember even these assumed identities?! Everything ends in deep slumber because the mind disappears in the lap of ignorance and you do not remember anything. And say, if your *prāna* were to exit the body in the state of deep sleep, you won't even realise that you are dead! That is why the wise say that one should not die in sleep. One should be aware that the body is dying. Thus it is very important that you don't die in sleep. This is because such is the deep rooted attachment with body that the *Jiva* will not be able to accept death of the body and hence will be stuck in limbo.

Owing to the countless *samskārās* and *vāsanās* in the mind, the mind keeps engaging with the sensory world trying to fulfil its desires. Thus you keep on performing *karmas* and every *karma* bears a fruit, a result. You plant one seed which grows into a tree. But how many fruits does the tree bear? Numerous. And how many seeds are borne by the fruits? Countless. And each seed has the potential of growing into an independent tree and then each tree will produce further fruits and seeds..! Likewise, although you perform a single *karma*, that one seed of *karma* will fructify into thousands of fruits and each fruit, in turn, contains thousands of seeds which can each develop into a new tree. Let me exemplify this for you. Say your mind is desirous of just one thing and that is to get married. So, there exists just one desire of marriage. Now you start planning. Money is needed, a house is needed, a job is needed so that you can live with your prospective bride or groom, as the case may be. Thus you get a job, take loan for a house, look for a suitable partner and finally set a date for the marriage. Meanwhile you need to take another bank loan so as to take care of the marriage costs. Well, it is another matter that after marriage this cost just keeps on spiralling out of control – what with the wife's clothes, jewellery, expensive outings, holidays, cinema. And then soon children arrive on the scene and then that is it, for you want them to have the best food, the best education, the best healthcare, the best amenities and the list goes on and on. All this palaver resulting from just one desire!

One desire begets thousands more. One fulfilled desire progenerates into a chain of countless desires. Thus *karma* keep on happening and every *karma* bears a fruit which has the seeds of further *karma*. Your past, your present and your future are all linked with each other. Your *sanchit karma* gave you this life and these life experiences. But the sum total of *sanchit karma* is immensely vast and only a few of your desires will get fulfilled in this lifetime.

Moreover, with every passing moment, newer desires are getting added to the already endless list of desires, isn't it?

Can you see how widespread is this mesh of desires? Multitudinous *samskārās* in the background and then on top of that myriad of newer *vāsanās* and desires keep getting added on from moment to moment! So how many lifetimes will be needed for the fulfilment of this never ending list of desires?! The phenomenon of *karma* is indeed mind bogglingly complex. Your *sanchit karma* has a bearing on every aspect of your life – be it wealth, health, education, relatives, death of your relatives and so on and so forth. There is absolutely nothing in your life which is not connected to your own past *karma*.

So we revert back to the question: How can one become free from the bondage of *karma*? Is it not possible that no *samskārās* are formed in the mind at all? Well, the sense organs are continually open to the sensory world. Thus sensory information will keep on getting registered in your mind. But the way out is to create a distance between your mind and 'you'. In this context, you need to understand what 'past' means. Past does not mean just your previous lifetime or your childhood or last year, so to say. The previous moment is your past now. Every passing moment becomes your past; every moment yet to come is your future; present moment is your present. Thus if you do virtuous deeds in the present moment your future will accordingly be pleasant, but if you commit sinful acts in the present moment your future is going to be hellish, damned. *Pāpa* and *punya* i.e. acts of merit and demerit, virtuous acts and sinful acts are both taking place in your present. And with every passing moment, your present is turning into your past and the next moment is your future. Your past is affecting your present, and your present will influence your future. Thus life is not linear, but rather it is circular. Body is born, grows old, then dies; again a new body is born, ages, dies and the cycle goes on.

And you simply cannot refrain from doing actions in the present. As long as there are *samskārās* in your mind, so will *vāsanās* be, and so will be a myriad of desires which will keep translating into *karma* and every *karma* will result in a fruit, a consequence – both visible and invisible. The *punya* and *pāpa karmas* that you have performed become your past. But what is *punya* and *pāpa* anyway? The definition is not limited only to virtuous or sinful deeds respectively but if we delve deeper, at the level of the mind, then whatsoever that generates pain and suffering in the mind is *pāpa*. Understand this carefully for I am not referring only to malevolent actions (like raping, plundering, stealing, murdering etc).

You see a branded watch and your mind says, 'I want to own that watch'. But you cannot afford it, so you are pained – remember, for you, this too is *pāpa*. Someone steals a loaded suitcase of a fellow passenger and then makes use of its items. Now, with how much genuine happiness will the burglar actually enjoy the stolen items – this is worth pondering over. He knows very well that it is not his hard earned possession, and simultaneously he is also apprehensive that someday he may get caught, thus the fear of impending punishment and social defamation. But before we go any further let me clarify that I am not talking about hard core criminals who have no iota of conscience in them. Such devils derive great pleasure in killing, raping and that is why they commit such heinous crimes. Such people have become so deeply entrenched in animalistic tendencies that they simply cannot be labelled as human beings. This knowledge is not intended for those who are sadistic, masochistic, misanthropes and psychopaths! After all, would Hitler accept that *pāpa* means pain? The one who slaughtered lakhs of Jews in the most inhuman way in the concentration camps – can this knowledge be meant for such misanthropic psychopaths? This discussion is aimed at those who are essentially human, who are trying to understand humaneness, who are trying to evolve, to rise above baser instincts, who are trying to eradicate their ignorance.

So with this clear understanding, we move back to the definition of *pāpa* which means pain and suffering. If you think about it, why do people commit sinful acts? It is due to their underlying selfishness which in turn is a product of ego. Thoughts such as, 'How dare he say that to me', 'How can his car be flashier than mine', 'How can his house be grander than mine, now I have to belittle him, I have to put him down only then will I be happy' – this anger, this thought process is resulting from an inflated ego. Such an egotistic person is self-centred and does not act rationally, for his actions are motivated by a desire to validate his ego. So he will do anything and everything to boost his ego.

Such an egocentric, desire-driven mercenary will have no qualms even in stamping his dead father's finger print on to a document so that he can acquire the father's wealth. Someone gets his father killed for the sake of wealth, some woman gets her husband murdered for the sake of money, a man kills his brother over property dispute – all these gruesome incidents flashed in the media are, in effect, a reflection of the perpetrator's ego. These egomaniacal people are so self-centred that their selfishness puts blinkers on their intellect such that they cannot think rationally and end up executing preposterously senseless actions. All such actions that occur when the intellect has been shrouded by selfish egocentricity are known as *pāpa karma* and these result in pain and suffering – both to the perpetrator and also the victim.

Punya karma, on the contrary, refers to all those actions which result in joy and happiness. Now interestingly enough, these actions too, are motivated by a selfish desire – the desire to be happy, to get good fruits of *punya karma.* Thus people go on pilgrimage so that they can accumulate virtuous *karmas* which in turn will bequeath auspicious fruits. In a similar vein, people give alms so that they get some good fruit in return, driven indeed by selfish, self-centred desires. And as we have discussed earlier, it is the underlying ego which leads to self-centred actions.

Many such people do charity so that others hail them as great philanthropists; they go to temples and gurudwaras every day so that everyone respects them for being very religious – ego-boosting exercises! Several years ago, I had just finished delivering a discourse in a small *ashram* and people were coming forward to 'pay respects'! One old woman flung a ten rupee note in my lap. When I opened my eyes, she demanded to be given back 8 rupees, for she wanted to give only 2 rupees but didn't have the change. Amused, I asked her to keep her ten rupees, for I was no cashier sitting there to deal with money! But the woman kept on insisting that I take 2 rupees from her. Now why was she being so adamant about it? This is because she must have heard somewhere that it is *punya karma* to offer money to sages, which results in auspicious fruits – thus her greed for the fruit was propelling her to keep on flinging the ten rupee note towards me! The sum and substance of the matter is that be it *punya* or *pāpa karma* – they are both driven by selfish motives propelled by the ego.

When you carry out *pāpa karma,* you inflict pain and suffering not only upon yourself but also upon others. Thus they are like iron shackles binding and fettering you. It is said that once King Dhritrashtra asked Sri Krishna, 'Why was I born blind?' The Lord replied, 'This is because in one of your previous lifetimes, you had, albeit playfully, pierced the eyes of an insect. And as a consequence of that action, you are born blind in this lifetime.' But it is very difficult for ordinary folk to accept that their misfortunes are a result of their own actions. Furthermore, they suffer more by obsessing over what they have or haven't received in their lives.

A sage, a man of realisation, a devotee on the other hand, never gets agitated by any event occurring in his life. Surdas, when asked, whether he had performed *pāpa karma* in his past, as a result of which he was born blind, he replied, 'I don't know if being blind is a result of any previous *pāpa karma*. All I know is that I am very grateful to my Lord for making me blind because otherwise my mind would have again got entangled in this phenomenal world. Whereas now all that my mind can think about is nothing but my beloved Lord.' Self-realised, hallowed beings are desire-less; they have no desires whatsoever. In the third chapter, verse thirty-seven, Sri Krishna says:

kāma eṣa krodha eṣa rajo-guṇa-samudbhavaḥ
mahāśano mahā-pāpmā viddhy enam iha vairiṇam

It means, 'Desires borne from *rajoguna* transform into anger and this is the all-devouring sinful enemy in this world. These *rajoguna*-borne desires propel people to carry out the worst possible sinful acts leading to immeasurable pain and suffering. The *Jiva* howls under the onslaught of these evil desires but still refuses to give them up! So, where is the pain, the suffering coming from? From your own desires. You get caught up in a mesh created by your own desires and suffer immensely as a result, in spite of this you still don't relinquish your desires.

King Bhartrhari had relinquished his palace, his wealth, his opulent life and donning the garb of a monk, he started living atop a mountain. He would spend his days in spiritual practices. One day, whilst he was meditating, he heard some noise and opened his eyes. He saw something red, glistening a few hundred yards away. Immediately a thought occurred, 'well, that could be a rare ruby.' After all, he had seen loads of precious gems in his palace. So, giving up his meditation, he hurriedly walked down the steps and looking sideways to ensure no one was watching him, he put his hand down to grab the item, but instead of a precious stone, it turned out to be red, sticky pulp residue of someone who had just spit a chewed betel leaf! Bhartrhari was shocked with the state of his own mind. Having left his palatial life aspiring spiritual ascension, the mere sight of a gem-lookalike had made him give up his meditation? The remorseful, ashamed King wept inconsolably rebuking his mind for having fallen prey to the *vāsanā* which made him give up his meditation and all for what – a mere facade of a gem? Later, he went on to write in a book (*vairagyashatak*): Even the greatest of renunciates can fall into the clutches of desires; such deep rooted is the bondage of *vāsanās*, the bondage of *pāpa karmas*. Indeed *pāpa karmas* bind you in a vice like grip; they drown you as would a heavy stone.

Now, the one who carries out *punya karma* may not harm others but he cares less about others, as his focus is entirely upon his selfish gains. His interest comes ahead of others. Such people are always keen on performing virtuous acts for they are desirous of the auspicious fruits. Furthermore, they want to show off their magnanimity to others. Thence, you will see that on occasions like *Mouni Amavasya, Ganga Dussehra,* people throng to Haridwar just to take a dip in the river. They give out alms, feed Brahmins, running hither to thither – all for the sake of accumulating *punya karma*! Remember, *punya karma* too is bondage, for it is a shackle that further bolsters, further reinforces the ego. 'There cannot be a greater altruist, a greater philanthropist than I', the *punya karmi* proclaims – directly or indirectly! Thus the crux of the matter, the bottom line is that both, *pāpa* and *punya karma*, bind you – they put fetters around your feet and shackle you in bondage. And both inflate your ego, making you egotistic. Yes, doers of *pāpa karma* also brag about their actions – openly or to a select few. Thus a successful shoplifter will boast about his 'achievement' to his friends. Likewise, many people proudly declare what all they managed to 'pick' from their hotel rooms without getting caught! Thus, whether it is *pāpa* or *punya karma,* either way the ego gets boosted.

In the above mentioned verse, Sri Krishna says that desires

are borne of *rajoguna*. If fulfilled they give rise to greed, and if unfulfilled they lead to uprising of anger. Thus he, whose mind becomes desire-less, he alone can be freed from the bondage of *punya* and *pāpa*. So, if you want to be freed from the bondage of *karma*, the mind needs to be in a state of equanimity and dispassion. And know that a disciplined life is the harbinger of dispassion. But what does a disciplined life entail? It involves a diligent practice of *pratyāhāra* (the fifth step of *ashtānga yoga*) – withdrawing the sense organs from the sensory world, not allowing the senses to wander in the objective world, bringing the senses back to their root.

Pratyāhāra is possible only for the one whose body is disciplined through the practice of *yoga āsanas*. And to be able to pursue practices dedicatedly, disciplined life is a pre-requisite, for which the performance of *nitya karma* becomes absolutely imperative. The foremost of this is to get up early in the morning, pursue your spiritual practices and then repeat them again in the evening. This includes the practice of *āsanas* and *prānāyama*. The one who practices *prānāyama,* his mind will invariably become calm and collected. But for this, one first needs to master *āsanas*. And the earlier one starts, the better – in fact, once a child reaches the age of 12 years, he or she should be introduced to *yoga āsanas*. Since the body is flexible, the child learns and masters the *āsanas* easily.

Disciplined life commences with the practice of *āsanas*, for *yoga āsanas* impart stability not only to the body but also to the mind. Then, when one sits for *prānāyama,* it further calms and stills the mind. Now, when the practitioner interacts with the world, the speed with which the mind gets involved in the world reduces automatically. Say you have had a sumptuous meal at home and you are completely satiated with the delicious food; then you go out for a stroll and happen to see several food stalls decorated with all kinds of savouries and sweets – will you be interested? No, because you are already satiated. On the contrary, the day you go out on an empty stomach – your eyes will see nothing but the food stalls and your mouth will start watering at the mere sight of food. Why? Because you are hungry!

When you start practicing *āsanās* and *prānāyama,* in effect, the mind's hunger for objects and relationships starts scaling down. The mind becomes calm, for it starts getting the joy from within which it has been seeking outside. Then why would it want to wander in the objective world anymore? When there are no desires in the mind, where does the question arise of any *karma* happening? And thus ends the loop of *agāmi karma.* When one perfects the practice of *prānāyama,* with the perfection of *pratyāhāra*, it opens the gates to the next stage viz *dhāranā.* And with this, the power of visualisation becomes so strong that one can get mental *darshan* of whosoever you want, be it Shiva or Rama or Krishna – one-dimensional thoughts get transformed into multidimensional images. When *dhāranā* matures, it evolves into *dhyāna*, and matured *dhyāna* culminates into *samādhi.* And all *sanchit karma* get incinerated in the state of *samādhi.* What this means is that just as roasted seeds cannot sprout; likewise, burnt out *sanchit karma* too cannot give fruits anymore. Then all that is left in such a seeker's life are his *prārabdha karma phala* – the fruits that he has to bear in this lifetime.

Now some scriptures say that after attaining *samādhi*, one has to take on three more births. Why? For the completion of his *prārabdha karma;* the arrows which have left the bow, that force will fructify and it is said that three lifetimes are needed for the exhaustion of the force of *prārabdha.* But the three lifetimes will be replete with immense joy. Why? This is so because from *sabeej-samādhi* to *nirbeej-samādhi* to self-realisation he will just keep on evolving. After all, the body has a finite lifespan, as determined by your *prārabdha*. Thus the seeker practices until the death of his body and then another birth happens wherein he continues on his path of evolution. In fact, he will be born to virtuous, spiritually inclined parents and right from his childhood, his environment will be conducive for his spiritual ascension. Thus the journey recommences from the point it was left in the previous lifetime. The twentieth verse from chapter four of the Bhagavad Gita states:

tyaktvā karma-phalāsaṅgaṃ nitya-tṛpto nirāśrayaḥ
karmaṇy abhipravṛtto 'pi naiva kiñcit karoti saḥ

The one who has abandoned all desires as well as attachment to fruits of actions, ever-content and dependent on nothing, despite being engaged in actions such a man of perfection, in essence, doesn't do anything at all.

Now, why has he abandoned the desire for fruits of actions? Because there is no 'doer' left in him at all. When you identify with the mind i.e. with the notion 'I am the mind', in effect, you become the doer and when you perform actions with the attitude of being the doer-of-actions then you will also have to be the bearer-of-the fruits of the actions. The doer will have to be the bearer, irrespective of whether the fruits are of *pāpa* or *punya karma*. The one who abandons, who gives up the notion of being the doer, such a person has no more attachment to the fruits of the actions. What's more, such a being is ever content, ever satiated for he is established in his real Self. And his mind is not dependant on anyone or anything. Now compare this with the status of your mind – on how many things and beings is it dependant? 'I will be happy when I have those objects', 'I will be happy when I have a big house, 'I will be happy when I marry that person', the list of dependency, the list of expectations is endless.

Recently a person was relating an incident. On her flight, there was an extremely wealthy tycoon who suffered a heart-attack when the plane was 35000 feet up in the air but nothing could be done about it. Now all the credit cards in his pocket notwithstanding, could all the wealth in the world come to his aid then? Fact of the matter is, no matter how rich you are, you cannot buy even one moment of life. Yet you keep on wasting your present moment by obsessing over people and objects!

Whereas Sri Krishna is saying that a *gyani*, a man-of-realisation, is not dependent on any one. You, on the other hand, are dependent on your spouse, your parents, your children – you cannot live without them, without your possessions and wealth – what all are you dependent upon?! My dears! Don't be emotionally dependent on anyone; don't harbour expectations from anyone.

Thus when *karmas* are performed without the notion of doership, without the attitude of being the doer, then they simply cannot bind you anymore. And in order to become ever content, not dependent on anyone, let me repeat the means of achieving this state: de-attachment, dispassion and vigilant witnessing. Be a witness of your mind – its thoughts, desires and emotions. Learn to objectify your mind i.e. witness your mind as an object which is distinct from you. For this, you will first have to start with your body i.e. witnessing your body separate from you. Now, if you are able to practice this in your life, then it will lead to a calm and collected mind within which *viveka* will blossom. *Viveka* is the discriminating faculty between what is real and what is unreal, what is eternal and what is perishable. And this will awaken only on a backdrop of *vairagya* (dispassion), de-attachment and non-dependence.

See, mere listening to these words is not going to make you enlightened. If only it did, by now thousands of listeners like you would have attained self-realisation just by listening to my words! So why does this not happen? It is so due to the lack of *vairagya* (dispassion) in your mind. And why is dispassion lacking? It is so because the mind is full of attachments, and you have not taken any efforts in awakening the mode of witnessing.

So it is indeed lamentable that you have been listening to me for well over ten years but still I see that your mind is full of desires and attachments; still there is no sign of awareness. Kabir says, 'if there is no yearning, no thirst, no love for the Lord, then you are a bull and not a human.' How can anyone enlighten a person who is a slave of his sense organs, whose mind is full of all sorts of attachments and desires? But yet, I continue with my *prārabdha karma* of preparing the soil of your mind so that when the soil becomes fertile, in at least some of you, then the seed of this knowledge will germinate.

To summarise: dispassion, de-attachment, awareness, detached witnessing fill your present with *gyāna, viveka* such that no longer will any action happen through the attitude of doership. And thus you will put a halt to the otherwise relentless loop of *karma*.

Verse twenty-one from chapter four of the Gita states:

nirāśīr yata-cittātmā tyakta-sarva-parigrahaḥ
śarīraṃ kevalaṃ karma kurvan nāpnoti kilbiṣam

A man of perfection who is bereft of desires and expectations, his mind and body controlled and perfectly balanced, he performs all necessary actions having given up all possessions and concept of ownership. Thus he incurs no sin.

An enlightened being's mind is not dependent on the world. His mind is empty of all desires and full of dispassion; he has relinquished the very thought of hoarding. Yes, he does perform actions but these are limited, only for the sustenance of the body. And whilst performing these actions nothing taints his mind. Actions happen through him, for there is no notion of being the doer of actions. Thus a seeker who keeps on evolving with the tools of dispassion, desireless-ness, expectation-less-ness, de-attachment, eventually reaches the stage of *samādhi* wherein all his *sanchit karma* get incinerated. Then no more *agāmi karma* and the present is replete with bliss, love, *dhyāna* (meditativeness) *gyāna* with no trace of any attachment or egotism – can the present be any more beautiful than this! Then whether the body takes another birth or not – it does not matter. The person becomes choiceless.

Now let me take up some questions regarding Karma.

Question: If we chop off a tree trunk, the tree will not fructify, likewise can we not chop off the sapling, the tree of *samskārās*?
Gurumaa: Well, you may cleave a tree trunk but as long as the roots are intact, the tree will regrow. And the same is true for *samskārās*. One has to roast the seeds of *samskārās*, only then can they be prevented from germinating. And this incineration is done by practicing the precepts of *ashtānga yoga* in the fire of *vairāgya*. By consistent, continual practice when one reaches the state of *nirvikalpa samādhi*, then all the *samskārās* as well as *sanchit karma* get completely burnt out. Regular practice, *vairāgya*, love for the Lord and steadfast faith in the Guru – these are imperative. And remember that as long as your mind is fixated upon this world of *māyā*, as long as your mind is entangled in this world of people and objects, it will be impossible for you to centre your attention unto the Lord. Then all that will happen is – driven by the force of your *vāsanās* you will be inextricably caught up in the vicious cycle of *karma* and will have to face their consequences.

Question: The mind keeps on thinking incessantly, and when I pay attention to the thoughts it leads to some or the other desire. What should I do?
Gurumaa: Well, my dear this is as good as asking I keep on picking hot coal, now what should I do to prevent it from burning my skin?! You say your mind keeps on thinking, but does your mind have an existence independent of you? Thus all it means is that you have no

command over your mind. If someone says, 'I don't want to die but cannot prevent myself from drinking poison' – what will you say to such a looney?! What can anyone else do about this dilemma? If you don't want to die then don't drink the poison and vice versa – where is the question of seeking help from others? It is your mind that is raising desires. If they are fulfilled, it will lead to greed, and if not it will lead to anger and frustration – if you still haven't understood this then keep on playing the game of desires!

Question: If you reap what you sow then what is the role of *prāyaschit karma*, for the seed has already been sown?
Gurumaa: See, *prāyaschit karma* is where you are greatly disturbed and remorseful for an action that has happened through you. And you strongly feel that you shouldn't have done that deed. Slapping someone and then saying sorry – this is not *prāyaschit karma!* It is about sincerely feeling repentant about what you have done and wanting to rectify it. Say a man kills someone and then he profoundly regrets his action. Now, what can he do to absolve himself? Can he revive the dead man? No. But what he can do is to delve deep into his mind and look for the root of the poisonous *vāsanā* from which the anger arose, and then uproot it completely. This will ensure that never again does he carry out such vicious *karma*. But remember, *prāyaschit karma* cannot delete the fruit of the *karma*, in any way. It does not give you a clean chit, but yes it certainly enables you to cleanse the filth underlying the deeper layers of your mind.

The next part of this question pertains to *dhrida* and *adhrida karma*. Now this is a very vast and complex topic. But generically speaking, actions leading to someone's death or damaging someone's dignity or verbal disparagement of a sage, a guru, a *sādhu*, a devotee, a *yogi*, or physically harming such hallowed beings are examples of *karmas* which cannot be changed; their

fruits are unalterable and hence are known as *dhrida karma.*
Adhrida karma, on the other hand, is done unintentionally i.e. out
of ignorance but which don't lead to any harm to a person's life or
dignity. When you slander a sage, he does not retaliate and such
is the force of *prakriti* that the consequence comes back to you
straightaway. When you insult ordinary people, on the other hand,
they will counter your one insult with many more! So the account
gets settled. But a master doesn't accept your *karma* and thus it
returns to you like a boomerang. Anyway, why worry about what is
dhrida and what is *adhrida karma* – just focus on refraining from
doing *pāpa karma* (anything that leads to turmoil, turbulence, pain
or pollutes your mind).

Question: I can see my desires and *vāsanās* but I am unable to do
anything about it. Please guide.
Gurumaa: See, I doubt that you are aware of your *vāsanās*. If
you can overtly see a fly in your coffee, will you still go ahead and
drink it? If you could indeed 'see' your *vāsanās*, you would most
certainly not want to hold on to them or pursue them any longer. As
far as desires are concerned, the fact that you have to look after this
body means that you will have to earn money, feed it, clothe it, keep
it healthy, thus wanting to do a job, wanting to have a house and
so on are legitimate desires. However, wanting a promotion soon,
being envious of a colleague who has got a promotion, wanting
a bigger office – if someone stresses over these things then even
doing a job becomes a noose around the neck!

Kabir Sahib, so very aptly, puts this as, "A great conniver, a
great con-artist is *māyā*. I have realised this veritable truth." Well,
this poor *Jiva* has indeed been bamboozled by the *māyā* of this
mind! The mind never shows you the dark face of desire. It never
reveals that getting entrapped in the web of desires is simply futile
– No Sir! The mind never lets you see this. It always shows you the

brighter aspect of things. But the irrefutable fact is that if you keep on clinging to your desires, you end up suffering. But if you enjoy diving in the swamp of desires, what can I do about that?!

People often ask me, 'in spite of listening to so many of your discourses, why are attachments still there in my mind?' See, the basic, the instinctive need of mind is to be attached to something or the other. And in essence, it wants to be anchored to the Lord but because you have not united your mind with the divine, which is why it gets hooked on to the mother, father, spouse, children, uncles, aunties, friends, neighbours and the like. Then what can the wretched mind do? It simply makes do with whosoever and whatsoever it comes across. You forget that you will not gain anything by investing your mind and time in these fickle relationships.

You don't use your intellect, your *viveka* (sense of discrimination), that is why your attachments persist; they linger on and on. Let's suppose you had become so attached to the seat you occupied on the train or bus on your journey to the ashram that you refused to let go of it and keep sitting. What would have happened then? The public transport officials would have dragged you out, what else! Likewise, here you go on repeating 'I cannot live without my mother, without my wife, without my children...' But there comes the grim reaper (agent of death!) and drags you away in a jiffy. Neither your wife, your parents or your children will be able to prevent the exit of your *prāna*. Then who can you really claim to be 'mine'? But because people don't have this *viveka*, they keep on committing this grave mistake of getting attached to people and objects. And then keep on repeating this mistake again and again and yet again...

An Englishman travelled a great distance to meet a Zen master. The last leg of his journey involved climbing a steep mountain on a rugged pathway. He spent some time with the master and as the sun set, he took his leave. The master took his lamp and guided the Englishman up to the pathway. And then he started returning to his monastery. The alarmed fellow falteringly asked, 'How will I see the path in the dark without the lamp O master?' To which the master calmly replied, 'I had lit my own lamp and so should you. Your path will not get illuminated by my lantern. You will have to light the lamp of your wisdom.' Thus use your *viveka*. Before wishing for anything, contemplate if the object of your desire will actually fulfill you – whether it will help or hinder your spiritual journey. Don't rush into things. Learn to put a brake to your mind. But he alone can do this, who has received the training to do so. And what is this training? Your spiritual practice! In the absence of this training, you will be a slave to your mind, wanting everything that the senses perceive.

The other day, a lady brought along her twin girls, who were around 2 years old. I offered them a platter of sweets. It was amusing to see that they grabbed the sweets, trying to stuff their tiny hands with as many as they could. But because they couldn't grab them all, they started crying. More so, one of them stuffed the sweets in her mouth - wrapper still intact – and couldn't get her teeth into the chocolates! The body may be young, but the mind is ancient; thus its tendencies are the same old ones! The greed in their minds was pushing them to grab, snatch and hoard. The body changes but not the mind. The same afflictions, the same filth of greed, lust, envy, anger, egotism! They proved to be your nemesis in your earlier births and yet again you are ruining your life by burning in their fire? I see this drama every day! Irrespective of whether the body is that of a 6 month old baby or a child or an adult, every *Jiva* carries its *vāsanās* with it.

So, the crux of the matter is that if you want to break free of your age-old, archaic, error-prone living, then you will have to change your present by bringing spiritual practices on the forefront. The one who has a disciplined life, a disciplined mind along with virtues of de-attachment, dispassion and discrimination, keeps on ascending the spiritual ladder, culminating into a state of self-realization. That is when all *sanchit karma* get burnt and one is finally freed from the otherwise relentless, inexorable cycle of *karma*.

Chapter-10

THE ASTROLOGY CONNECTION

'What did I ever do to deserve this suffering in my life?' – this is a universal grievance. People don't want to accept that they are bearing the fruits of their own *karma*. It is their own past actions that are responsible for all that is happening in their present. Thus they keep seeking remedies from so-called astrologers. Astrology is undoubtedly a great science; after all it is a part of the hallowed *Vedas*. But it is hard to find genuine, knowledgeable astrologers - this is not surprising, given that it takes at least thirty years of rigorous study along with regular spiritual practise. On the other hand, there is no dearth of self-proclaimed 'astrologers' who claim to offer remedies for all your problems. They claim that they can change your present with the use of some stones, some crystals and such like. Little do these charlatans know that the fruits of *karma* are of three types: *dhrida* (unalterable), *adhrida* (possibility of alteration), and the third is a mixture of the two viz. *dhrida-adhrida* wherein a part is unalterable and the other part is changeable.

Many people ask whether the 'remedies' offered by these astrologers work. Well, they act upon your mind. The faith in the remedy strengthens your mind such that it is able to endure the fruits of *karma* one is receiving in the present. As mentioned above, modifications are possible in some part of *adhrida karma*, but the important question is: Who can bring about these alterations? It can only be done by the one who knows the process inside out. For example, an astute astrologer has a deep insight and by seeing the position of planets he can gauge the status of Saturn, its relationship with the moon, its friendly and unfriendly planets, the *mahādashā* and so on. There are four *dashās* functioning at any given time: the *mool* or main *dashā*, and the others are known as *antar*, *pratyantar* and *sookshma dashā*. The astrologer first checks out the *mooldashā* and then sees the other three *dashās*. This is followed by a detailed study of the planets, their relationship with other planets, whether they are friendly or unfriendly, what are the cross connections and so on. It is indeed a complex science which involves a lot of calculations. Thus it is absolutely imperative that one knows the precise time of birth otherwise the horoscope will be wrong. The astrologer assesses the position of the planets in degrees, the longitude and latitude of the place you were born, but many so-called astrologers are oblivious of this knowledge and hence don't do any of these calculations.

These swindlers have made a mockery of this great science and abuse it to fool people and make money. This is indeed a travesty of this invaluable, priceless science, stemming from none other than the great *rishi* Parashar (sage Vyasa's father). Now would the great *rishi* have written the scripture for material gains? 'My business is not doing well, so what remedy can I go for?', 'My wife is not bearing a son, what remedy should I opt for?' – did the hallowed sage write the text for these reasons?! Fact of the matter is that astrology aims at making the mind free of desires. It is meant for empowering one to accept his *prārabdha karma* composedly. It is intended for making people aware of the consequences of *karma* such that they do not get trapped in the loop of *agāmi karma*. But such is the woeful travesty of this esteemed science that these days it is being sold for pennies – be it the fellow with his parrot on the road-side or the fortune teller marketing through the medium of television or the sophisticated fellow making computerised horoscopes. All have made a money-spinning business out of this noble science!

The scriptures clearly state that the science of astrology is not meant for making money; it is not a commercial business. Secondly, the original scriptures do not talk about remedies at all. Mythology cites a story in this context: It is said that once *Shani* (Saturn) went to Lord Shiva to warn him of his impending *dashā* of *Shani*. Lord Shiva was totally unperturbed. He told *Shani*, "Well, you do your job, I can't prevent you from doing what you do." Devi Parvati got worried. But the Lord pacified her saying that there was a way by which he could ensure that *Shani* bears no influence on him. Thus, he went into a cave atop a remote mountain and sat there in deep meditation for a good 12 years – that was the duration of *Shani's dashā*. When he emerged from the cave, he found *Shani* waiting outside. Lord Shiva said, "I did manage to escape your influence, didn't I?" To which *Shani* replied, "Dear Lord, but didn't you stay in total seclusion, mind cut away from the world, all this time for 12 years? Whose influence was that if not mine!"

The story is not to be taken literally but it does have a moral which is that if Lord Shiva could not escape the influence of *Shani*, what chance on earth do you have in doing so?! The other important interpretation is that just like Lord Shiva did, whenever faced with *Shani*'s *dashā*, you too should get absorbed in meditativeness and dissolve your mind in *mantra*. See, if your mind is full of ignorance, replete with desires, you will have to endure the influences exerted by the planets. He alone is spared, who is desire-less. When he doesn't sow seeds, what fruits will he reap then?

Your body is made as well as governed by the force of nature. And your mind has to bear the consequences of the actions done by your body. You may bribe human beings to escape loss or punishments but no bribery works in the realm of *karma*! This doesn't mean that remedies have no place or value. For example, say a person goes to his guru wailing that his times are not good. The master sees his astrological chart and, let's say, finds that *Shani*'s *dashā* is not good. Now, *Shani* is a worshipper of Shiva. Thus, the guru advises the grieving fellow to worship Lord Shiva – get up early in the morning, sit with spine straight and recite Shiva *mantra*, facing the north direction, and do the same in the evening. In addition, serve elders or needy, be charitable and donate alms. The follower asks, 'How long should I do this?' The guru says, 'Do it for 6 months.'

Now imagine this fellow's routine for six months – his life will be full of virtuosity, regular performance of spiritual practices, regular chanting of the Lord's name. And remember, the mind does not wander in sorrow as much as it does in happiness. Sorrow makes the mind contemplative such that worldly thoughts don't disturb as much when one sits for *mantra* chanting. *Mantra* acts as a shield. Thus the guru does not say, 'Don't worry, it will not rain.' Rather the guru advises, 'Keep your umbrella open, for then the rain will not drench you.' Likewise, astrological remedies run on a parallel to this example. They don't claim that there will be no rain of suffering, rather the remedy tells you to be ready with your shield, your umbrella, your raincoat.

Thus, a fellow who would otherwise steal, even from a beggar, is now being generous, chanting *mantras*, serving, giving alms – who has brought about these changes? Will you still say that the fellow is going through a bad phase because of *Shani*?! The ones who have taken refuge in their master, their times can never be bad. Why? This is because by continual contemplation, *mantra* chanting, acts of virtuosity and prayer, their mind gets so empowered that no calamity can faze them anymore.

Angulimaal was a notorious plunderer and murderer who had killed ninety-nine men. He would chop off their fingers as a souvenir, wearing the finger-garland around his neck. But a chance meeting with Buddha transformed him radically such that he became a *bhikshu* (a monk) and Buddha named him Ahinsak. After several years of practice, Buddha asked him to go to a particular village and spread his teachings. But before he could do that, he had to answer Buddha's questions. The first question was, 'What will you do if people verbally abuse you?' Ahinsak replied, 'Dear master, I will put it aside knowing that it was just a string of words, no physical harm.' Buddha asked, 'But what if others physically assault you?' Ahinsak replied, 'Dear master, I will not retaliate because they would be hurting only this body, after all, I would still be alive.' Buddha countered, 'And what if they kill you?' Ahinsak replied, 'In that case, beloved master, I will be so grateful for their compassion for having relieved me of any possible desire-driven mistakes I could commit in the future.' Buddha exclaimed, 'Ahinsak! You have become an embodiment of compassion. I know now that you are most certainly the right person to spread my teachings.'

This is what remedies do! They make your mind stronger and empower you with endurance to bear with whatsoever is to come in your life. Through the process of observing austerities, chanting *mantras*, the person gets protected from his *adhrida* (alterable) *karma*. But remember that no one can save you from your *dhrida* (unalterable) *karma*. Otherwise the whole principle of *karma* will become baseless. Embezzle crores of rupees and then give away few lakhs to charity – will you be absolved of your crime? Kill thousands of people and then get a hundred *pundits* to do thousand times chanting of *mahamritunjaya mantra* – will that exonerate your heinous act? Thus the greatest teaching of the principle of *karma* is to become responsible i.e. to be responsible for your *karma* and face the consequences of your actions. And whilst enduring the fruits of your *karma*, pursue your spiritual practices in the present with *viveka* and *vairagya*. This is the way you will free yourself from the entanglement of *agāmi karma*. And whatever fruits are there in the present – a devotee, a seeker, a spiritual practitioner accepts these without any complaint. He remains equanimous in all conditions – be it happiness or sorrow he accepts his *prārabdha* graciously. This becomes possible because he has found the real source of joy, for he has realised that joy is not in people and things. As far as the world is concerned, you will keep receiving your share of pain and pleasure, as per your *prārabdha*. Your mother, father, brothers, sisters, uncles, children are all in your life for give and take, to settle the account of previous *karma*.

Your past was once your present and your future will one day become your present. In the present you are experiencing the consequences of your past actions, whilst at the same time you are performing new actions. Thus the cycle of *karma*, the cycle of time continues and will continue until a day comes when you decide, 'enough is enough, no more entanglement in the loop' – you resolve to change the present. But here again, this thought of changing the present will occur only to those who have accrued fruits of some *punya karma*. Otherwise, in the absence of fruition of some *punya karma,* even if you request someone to accompany you to *satsang*, he will snap at you saying, 'Are you mad? Why would I want to attend *satsang* when I can have a good time at the movies, the restaurant, shopping mall…?'

The problem is that your mind cannot stay without thinking. It will entertain either sinful or virtuous thoughts and act accordingly. As I have already explained, both *punya* and *pāpa karma* bind you, but as the quantum of *punya* increases, two rare events become possible in your life: meeting a sage, and listening to spiritual discourses. That is why one ought to refrain from doing *pāpa karma* and endeavour to do as much *punya karma* as possible. Think and contemplate upon that which is good. And refrain from slinging mud on others; neither speak ill of others nor listen. A wise person never taints his mind by vilifying others or listening to others' vilification. See, would you allow anyone to throw garbage in your lounge? Then why do you allow people to use your mind as their litter bin?! Elated by something, dejected by something; sometimes happy, sometimes sorrowful; already bogged down by old attachments but yet hell bent upon forming new attachments – what a lamentable, deplorable way of living!

How aptly Kabir Sahib puts it, "No more do I want to live in the world of this mind. Eyes, nose, ears, tongue, skin – all these senses keep running after objects and the diseased mind helplessly, compulsively follows them. But I have to pay for the *karma* performed by the *karma indriyas* (organs of motor activity) – the afflictions of anger, greed, lust, attachment, envy propel all kinds of *karma* but I am asked to pay the price for their deeds. Thus O Lord! Save me! For no longer do I wish to abide in the world of this mind." The day you too get fed up of this relentless rigmarole, you will desperately seek the way out and the heartening thing is that the one who seeks, finds. One most certainly does!

Chapter-11

REINCARNATION, KARMA & ASTROLOGY: THE INTERFACE

What is the science, the reality behind birth? It is the inexorable force of *karma* which propels the *Jiva* to take birth. The substratum of the mind is the *Chaitanya* (ever-knowing consciousness). And this gets reflected in an individual mind. It can be likened to say, the moon, its reflection in a body of water and the water – herein, the moon symbolises the *Ātman* or the real Self, the water represents the mind, and the reflection of the moon in the water, along with the moon and the water, is known as *Jiva*. At the time of conception, when the spermatozoon enters the ovum, at that very moment we can say that the *Jiva* enters the fertilised egg. See, when you flick the switch of a light bulb, within less than a fraction of a nanosecond, light comes on. It is with that very speed that energy of the *Jiva* enters the fertilised ovum, and from that point on the embryo starts growing. Now, just as electricity cannot enter a bulb wherein the filament has fused, likewise *Jiva* cannot reside in the body from where the mind has exited. That is why we declare the body as dead. Mind is like the tungsten filament in a bulb – if the filament does not work, neither will the bulb. The filament in the bulb of your body is the mind (to be precise it is the unit of mind-intellect-subconscious-ego). In the absence of this filament of mind, the *Jiva* cannot reside in the bulb of this body any more. Thus we can say that first the mind 'arrives', then the body starts getting formed.

Now, what is mind? Mind is your thoughts, your emotions, your *samskāras*, your *vāsanas* and your desires. Thus a mind which is full of *samskāras, vāsanas,* desires, exits the body at the time of death but the force of its *vāsanas*, its desires propels it towards a new gross body. And know that this is bound to happen; this process simply cannot be stopped. What's more, it doesn't matter if the propelling desires are innumerable or just a single, lone desire. That is the reason why some enlightened masters too take another birth, because of the underlying desire of wanting to help ignorant beings escape from the cycle of *karma*, just as they did. It is out of sheer compassion that they choose to be born again. The point to note is that even a sage is not born without any underlying desire. For example, my much endeared friend, Swami Buaji, lived until the age of 125 years. He was very active even at that age and had a strong desire to open an ashram in Bangalore to teach yoga. He wanted me to be there and join him in teaching, in eradicating others' ignorance. Thus I am absolutely certain that when he finds a suitable womb, which matches his calibre and with whom he has some *karmic* give and take, he will definitely return in the human form; he will certainly take another birth because of his desire. Now the question arises: How many desires do you have? Just know one thing that every birth is for the fulfilment of a desire!

From your letters I note that many of you are worried about how to ensure you don't perform *pāpa karma*. But it just shows that you are looking in the wrong direction. See, *karma* is indeed carried out by the body but the seed of *karma* originates in the mind. Thus instead of asking how to rectify your actions happening through the body, you ought to be asking how to reform the wayward mind, how to free the mind of lust, greed, attachment, anger, envy, egotism, so that neither do *vāsanās* form and nor do the consequential actions take place. Don't focus on actions – that is sheer foolishness. No action happens without a thought. First a thought arises, then it transforms into a resolve (*sankalpa*) and this then translates into a physical action. Thus your focus should be on your mind from where the force of desire arises, how to sort that – this should be your concern.

Your mind is full of countless desires. Some are visible to you and then are those you are not even aware of. The volcano of *vāsanās* is simmering inside, the seeds of innumerable *samskārās* are lying dormant in your mind and you have no clue about any of this. The seeds await the right conditions for germination. I know many women who are very spiritually inclined, very keen on following my teachings but their husbands are totally against it. Sometimes, they even thrash their wives for visiting the ashram. And occasionally it is the other way round – the husband wants to follow my teachings but the wife is dead against it. Now why is this so? This is because their mind is full of such deluded thoughts and caught up in the fetters of ignorance that they are unable to see the naked truth staring at them. Their *pāpa karma* ensure that they keep on wandering in this material world; they ensure that such folk don't get even to listen to a sage's words which would have otherwise shown them the way out of the bondage of *karma*.

Be it *pāpa* or *punya*, remember that *karma* is a force, a momentum. *Karma* is much more than just action – it is the physical execution of a thought. And when your body dies, the mind continues. It is the same mind that existed thousands of years ago. Body changes, but the mind remains the same! You may well have been a woman in some births, a man in others; what's more you would have been a tree, an insect, an animal in some previous lifetimes. With evolution, you acquired the human body. But gripped by ignorance and attachment your mind keeps on doing actions which are completely devoid of intelligence, *viveka* and meditativeness.

I know of a well-heeled, filthy rich business man who has all the money in the world. All he ever did in his life was start new businesses, make them bigger, purchase mansions, cars, literally rolling in money. But health-wise he has been steadily deteriorating. It started with mental problems which have now begun to manifest in his body. All the doctors in the world are unable to treat him and soon he will be helpless to feed himself, bathe himself, walk on his own. His father too suffered the same way. He too spent his entire life obsessing over money and then died a very distressing death, being bed-ridden for years with an untreatable chronic ailment. And this fellow is doing the same! The body has aged but the mind is the same. The darned mind makes you run after this material world like a headless chicken and then one day the body drops dead. But the mind stays as young as ever – the same *vāsanās*, the same desires and it is this force that chalks out the blueprint of your next life. Thus it is because of your *karmic* force that you are here on this planet. God hasn't sent you down! You have landed here because of the force of your own *karma*.

Now, the science of *karma* was studied and understood in-depth by our ancient sages, through the branch of astrology. As I already explained, astrology is meant for showing you the way out of the labyrinthine web of *karma*. It reveals that your present situation is a consequence of your own previous *karma*. And if you are the cause of your bondage, then astrology assures that you can become the cause of your liberation too.

Reverting to the *Jiva* and rebirth, the mind of the *Jiva* awaits the right condition to enter a fertilised egg. This is governed by the *karmic* accounts which the *Jiva* has to settle – this decides which womb is chosen. *Jiva's* mind is constantly being pushed and pulled by the torrent of desires. For example, a part of your mind may say, 'let's go to the pub and have a good time.' The other part however reminds you, 'people might see you there, hence best drink at home.' Push and pull! Mind of a young man goads him into visiting a brothel, and sometimes he does succumb to this desire. But at other times, he is torn by guilt and fear of being caught. Push and pull! Often the print and television media run stories of youngsters (and adults too) having been caught at some rave party. All of them have their faces covered up – I wonder whether such folk move around with a shroud in their pockets, always prepared in case they get caught and publicised in the media! One mind is pushing towards adultery, towards drug abuse, towards alcoholism and another part is raising cautionary thoughts. One mind says, 'let's go to the *shivir*', the other says, 'no way José!' Your *karmic* force is going to pull you towards the appropriate combination of parents. Yes, it is the force of your own *karma* which has chosen your current set of parents. Pieces of a jigsaw fit only in the correspondingly shaped cavity. You can't put a square unit into a circular space. Such is the corresponding, the complimentary relationship between your *karma* and your parents' *karma*. The fertilised egg produced by your father and mother provided the exact match for you to 'fit in' and thus you were born to them.

More often than not, a moribund person becomes unconscious just before death. And when the *prāna* exits the body in such a state, the *Jiva* doesn't realise that the body has died. It gets bewildered by seeing the wailing relatives, for it cannot understand why people are taking its body to the crematorium. It cannot comprehend that *prāna* has left the body, and it has been separated from the body. *Prāna,* senses of cognition (*gyāna indriya*), senses of motor activity (*karma indriya*) are all within the *Jiva* – hence the *Jiva* can see, can hear but because the body is no more, cannot speak, touch or perform any motor activity.

The Hindu religion advocates that a dead body should be cremated as soon as possible. One reason is to prevent decomposition of the cadaver, thus they put it on a funeral pyre (or electric cremator) soon before the body swells and gets infested with maggots. But there is another critical reason which is to make the *Jiva* realise that no longer does it abide in that body. So strong is the attachment with the body that many a times it does not understand that the body is dead; that no longer does the body belong to it. Thus it keeps hovering around the body. And may even try to re-enter the body, which is simply not possible. That is why our sages said that the sooner the body is cremated, the sooner the *Jiva's* attachment to the body snaps off. For only then will it move ahead on its journey towards next birth. But such is the attachment to the body that it sometimes delays the next birth, because the *Jiva* keeps on trying to re-enter the body somehow or the other. That which you refer to as ghost or spirit is the *Jiva* who hasn't as yet acquired a new body. It keeps lingering around the family, for its attachment prevents from letting go.

But having said so, you are not likely to 'see' these ghosts or spirits easily. This is because in comparison to ancient times, the vast majority of men and women these days are not virtuous – they are not spiritual aspirants, seekers, or devotees. Just for fulfilment of their biological needs such wanton folk rampantly indulge in sex, be it day or night. Thus, *Jivas* have ample opportunity to enter a fertilised egg and acquire a new body. And that explains the increasing number of malicious, nefarious, immoral people in this world. Such evil-minded *Jiva* are getting reborn sooner, thanks to the promiscuous, debauched societies world across. Our ancient sages had clearly delineated principles for married couples, specifically related to sex. Not only this, but astrological charts would also be seen to decide the day and time for the consummation of the marriage. The rationale behind this was that indulging in copulation only at certain auspicious moments would invite the birth of a virtuous, noble *Jiva*. By wanton, depraved and excessive, uncontrolled indulgence in sex, people are inviting evil-minded *Jiva* to be reborn. As I exemplified earlier, the body may be of a child but the mind is the same old mind. Angry, abusive, destructive – who teaches such children to be so violent? No need to teach, they bring it along with them, for the mind is the same, as vicious as ever.

But you folk have no clue about this. That is why when marrying off your children, all you see is that the girl should be beautiful and the boy should be moneyed. That's it, nothing else is needed! But because of this foolishness, you are in effect aiding the arrival of such vile, such vicious *Jiva* in human form. And that is why this era is known as *Kaliyuga* where people are rapaciously engaging in loveless sex and making it possible for the birth of malevolent *Jiva*. No devotion, no virtuosity, no spiritual inclination, no benevolence – will noble *Jiva* be born to such parents? That is why a great sage, a hallowed being, does not get reborn soon for there is no appropriately deserving womb, no rightful mother or father. On the other hand, those who are excessively *rajoguni, tamoguni,* sinners, get reborn very soon because there is no dearth of corresponding, like-minded parents. The entire society has become like that – it has become a norm of the times.

If you look at Shankaracharya's parents, on the other hand, you will find that before conceiving him, they had been worshipping Lord Shiva for sixty long years. Only then was Shankaracharya born to them. When Guru Teg Bahadur returned to a householder's life after twenty-six years of penance, it was then that Guru Gobind Singh was born. And like father, like son! But a mind brimming with *vāsanās* and desires doesn't have the privilege of choice. Such *Jiva* don't choose where to be born, rather their *karmic* forces push them into a new birth. Sometimes it is seen that an evolved, virtuous

Jiva gets born to parents who did not match its calibre, who did not deserve it. Often such children die within a span of eight years because the environment is not suitable for their spiritual ascension.

A life led in the absence of spiritual practices means that a state of unconsciousness envelops the *Jiva* a few hours before death. And depending upon its *karmic* force, the *Jiva* gets propelled into another birth. Death is the biggest surgery you will ever have, for therein not one or two or three organs are removed, rather the entire body gets changed. And as there is unconsciousness at the time of death, thence there is unconsciousness at the time of birth too. Thus know that you haven't chosen your parents, rather in your unconsciousness, your *karmic* force guided you into this current birth. You have landed here, in this form, in these circumstances so that you can bear the fruits of one part of your *sanchit karma* i.e. your *prārabdha*. On top of that, new *karma* are happening every moment because you don't understand your mind, you don't want to understand your mind, and you don't want to come out of its clutches. That is why the *Jiva* is trapped in the cycle of *karma*, the cycle of time.

So the thing you ought to remember is that astrology lies at the root of the principle of *karma*. Astrology is meant for comprehending the depths of the philosophy of *karma*. That is why astrology is deemed as an integral part of the *Vedas*, and before reading the Upanishads sages would ask their disciples to first study and understand the intricacies of astrology. Sanskrit, astrology, ayurveda would be taught first. And once these were comprehended, the student's mind would become calm, unruffled, for when one understands that one's own *karma* is the causative factor for present situation then where is the question of complaining, grumbling anymore? The being realises that he simply cannot blame anyone else, not even God, for his current predicament.

Astrology is the science of planets. It encompasses the nine planets of the solar system as a means to study life. The principle of *karma* forms the basis of astrology. It can be said that the science that dissects the connection, the influence of the nine planets on you, is known as astrology. Saturn, the outermost planet, impacts your *karma*; it can be likened to a judge. Mythology regards *Shani* or Saturn as the son of Yama, the God of time. This is of course a language of symbolism. What this means is that everything is existing in time. And who perceives time? It is the mind. And the mind itself is being guided by *vāsanās*. Every seed of *vāsanā* is going to germinate in time and the fruit will come to you, also in time. Furthermore, every fruit has thousands of seeds which will again fructify in time. The entire game is indeed of time!

Saturn is a heavenly body, the outermost planet, having a great impact on your life. And this should not be surprising, given that even the sun exerts such a profound effect on your life – its far off distance from the earth notwithstanding. If the sun were ever to collapse, this earth will be detrimentally cooled several hours before the incident would actually happen. Saturn also refers to *kāl*, time. And you cannot deny that everything is happening in the framework of time. Thus know that *Shani* is a force which is present not only in the form of a planet, but in effect it abides in your mind, in your body. *Shani* is the *Jiva's*, the mind's force of *karma*. It is the cause of all your *karma*. Similarly, *Bṛhaspati* or Jupiter is the source of your sense of 'being'. 'I am' – this perception, this notion of your intellect is because of Jupiter. And it is because of the 'sense of existing' that the *Jiva* thinks, wants and seeks to experience the sensory world. On the other hand, Mars or *Mangal* relates to your body, its energy. Interplay of the planets (because of *karma)* causes the *Jiva* to take birth on this earth. Thus, by virtue of the *karmic* force of the *Jiva*, Saturn ensures its birth, the sense of 'I am' comes from Jupiter, and Mars endows it with a body. It's all a game of the planets!

After all, where will your notion of 'I am' be when you die? Senses, mind, body, *prana* integrated – 'I am'; senses, mind, body, *prana* disintegrated – nowhere will this 'I' be found! What is this 'I' of yours anyway? One dose of anaesthesia and whoosh goes your 'I'! Do you know where you are in deep sleep? Thus, your notion, your sense of 'I am' is also because of the planets, so is your mind and body. The body, *Jiva* and *karma* – these three are but a play of the planets!

The moon is the causal factor of your mind. It exerts a tremendous influence over your mind and now science too has accepted this fact. Despite being so far away, the full moon causes a surge of high tidal waves in the oceans. If this is its influence on massive oceans, then imagine the moon's effect on your body, seventy percent of which is constituted of water. There is indeed a very deep connection. Gautama Buddha was born on a full moon day, attained enlightenment on a full moon day and left his body on a full moon day. How can anyone say there is no relation?! It is said that this entire universe originated from *Ishwara's Māyā* and the mind is regarded as the child of *Māyā*. And the moon has a causal link with the mind. Just as the moon waxes and wanes, so does your mind, doesn't it? Sometimes happy, sometimes sad; agitated at times, calm at other times – waxing and waning just like the moon. So, mind from the moon, *Jiva's* 'sense of existing' from Jupiter, body from Mars and *karma* from Saturn – this completes the full package! Who are you? Body, mind, *karmic* force and the sense of 'I am'. Are you anything more, anything other than this?! The notion of *Ātman*, *Paramātman* is sheer gobbledegook for you, because these are just words you have heard or read. They don't mean anything to you experientially.

Your existence is your body, your sense of 'I am' and your mind. And linked to your mind is also the planet Venus or *Shukra*. This planet signifies your creativity – the *Jiva* now creates a playground for itself. Venus means material enjoyment. Senses are needed for the fulfilment of mind's desires. It is through the medium of the cognitive senses that you are forever looking for the best things to eat, the best scenes to see, to best things to feel – these are the mind's desires and they are fulfilled via the senses. So, Venus entails sensory pleasure. But interestingly enough, all creative arts are also because of Venus, be it dance, music, sculpting, painting or any other creative art.

To re-iterate: *Karma* from Saturn, mind from Moon, body from Mars, the sense of 'I am' from Jupiter and material enjoyment from Venus. Thus starts the game of sensory indulgence. The moment the mother's nipple is offered to the new born, it immediately starts suckling at her breast. Now, who has taught the neonate to do so?! The body may be of a new born but the mind can perceive the body's hunger and thus even with closed eyes it is able to find the mother's breast and suck the milk. As the baby cannot speak, everytime the body is hungry, the baby informs the mother of its hunger by crying. Thus material enjoyment starts right from the moment of birth. At birth the baby knows how to suckle the mother's breast, then as it grows older, it starts playing with toys labelling them as 'mine'. As a child it is about 'I want toys', 'I want food', 'I want clothes'; growing into adolescence the desires move on to 'I want a girlfriend', 'I want a boyfriend...' Where are all these desires coming from? The mind! And that in turn is because of the *karmic* force i.e. due to Saturn.

Moving on to Mercury, this planet is linked with the onset of wisdom. And wisdom manifests only when *Jiva* transcends all materialistic, sensory gratification. Wisdom gets awakened only when one comes out of the attachment to sensory indulgence and gratification. Before this happens, it is the mind and only the mind. Do what the mind wants, don't do that which the mind doesn't want, befriend the one whom mind likes – everything is governed by the mind. What's more, it is your mind that has brought you to the ashram for this workshop! I cannot label this faculty as the intellect, because the intellect is awakened only when your pursuit of this material world comes to an end. Before this, what you label as intellect is nothing more than matured thoughts of the mind. You may well say that having considered several thoughts, my intellect decided upon one particular thought. No my dear! It is still your mind playing games.

Moving on to the next heavenly body the 'Sun' symbolising the *Ātman*. When the intellect becomes pure and sharp, then the glimpse of the real Self happens. Astrology regards the Sun as the cause of the body too. This is because the Sun is the source of energy pervading the body. In the absence of the Sun, let alone the body, this entire earth will become devoid of life. But the deeper essence of the Sun is that it is represents the *Ātman*. Let me exemplify this for you. Imagine the Sun personified as a man sitting on a chariot which is driven by a charioteer. The man's face is radiant and he is holding a mace, a conch, a lotus and a *chakra*. These four objects symbolise *sat* (truth), *chit* (ever-knowing consciousness), *ānanda* (bliss) and *vyāpaka* (all pervasive) respectively. And these are the attributes of *Paramātman*, your very essence. The chariot represents the body, the horses symbolise your senses, the reins are your mind and the charioteer is the intellect and the resplendent, beaming man sitting behind the charioteer symbolises the real Self, the *Ātman*. But in your case, the scenario is drastically different – the wheels of the chariot are broken, the horses are running amok, the reins are scattered and the charioteer is unconscious! And if the intellect is asleep and unconscious, who will know the real Self then? Thus, performing spiritual practices means repairing the wheels of this body through *āsanas*, commanding the horses (i.e. senses) by restraining them through the reins of the mind, and through awakened intellect restraining the mind from going wayward. And this awakening will happen through *satsang*. Thus take the medicine of awareness from your doctor (guru) to awaken the intellect – once this is awakened you will realise the real Self.

Moving on to *Rāhu* and *Ketu* – these are not planets. *Rāhu* is likened to fog or illusion whereas *Ketu* can lead to *moksha* (salvation). *Rāhu* has no head and *Ketu* has no body – this is of course, symbolic. Absence of head indicates absence of intellect and that is why one gets deluded. Intellect reflects *gyāna* and is represented by the Sun. So, the one whose Jupiter is defunct, whose Sun is defunct – how will he possess any intellect? And one gets to see so many such headless chickens, running helter-skelter – sensory gratification is all that they are interested in! *Rāhu* thus entails dense fog. Now, if you cannot see outside clearly on a foggy day, then will internal fog allow you to live well? Will it let you walk in the right direction? *Rāhu* also indicates sudden, rash, impetuous behaviour. It deludes, it illudes. 'This world is full of pleasure' – illusion. 'Drinking alcohol makes one merry' – illusion! 'Worry about your old age' – illusion. After all, who knows, you may die well earlier! *Rāhu* affects your mind and creates such illusions. 'The world is true' – illusion. 'Who has seen God, you duffer'- illusion.

Ketu can lead to salvation but is very mysterious too. *Rāhu* deludes you into getting more attached to this world, making you madly pursue one thing after the other. And then when you get the thing, your mind gets cut off from that object or being – this cutting off is the influence of *Ketu*. *Rāhu* entangles you, deludes you, illudes you and makes you run after this sensory world your entire life. You may have noted that old, elderly people often keep reminiscing about their 'golden olden times'. In fact often their sentences start with: 'In my times, things were so much cheaper, people were nicer but nowadays it is as hard to find a loving person as it is to find a needle in a haystack. I am so fed up with all my children; none of them is any good and what to say about the other half, the less said the better. I just want to leave everything and go far away...' *Ketu* thus cuts you off. You exert so much in forming relationships but when *Ketu* comes into the picture, then no one seems appealing any longer. Entire youth gets spent in the pursuit of wealth, fame and women and then when old age knocks on the door, the mind gets cut off from those very beings. But this does not mean that all the youngsters are sensory pursuers and all old people are full of *vairagya* – no way! Though the mind is cut off, as the mind is full of *vāsanās*, it keeps trying to bond with newer beings. For example, the grandfather fondly holds the grandson telling him, 'Your father turned out to be a rascal but you will look after me darling child, won't you?!' Full of *vāsanās* and shrouded by ignorance, the mind keeps on repeating the same mistakes again and again.

The doer is always the bearer. If the *Jiva* does *karma*, then it has to bear the results too. And thus the *Jiva* gets entangled in this never-ending cycle of doing *karma* and bearing its fruits. Every action leads to a chain of reactions. It is like a seed giving rise to thousands of fruits and then each fruit bearing manifold seeds which lead to multitudinous trees, countless fruits and countless seeds. What a deadly vortex, indeed! 'I am', 'I want' and 'I do deeds to acquire what I want' – *Jiva* thus becomes the doer and then inevitably has to bear the fruits and laments at having to do so. But yet, he doesn't realise the error of his ways and keeps doing something or the other with the motivation of getting pleasure, happiness from somewhere or the other. 'If not from here, then I will seek pleasure from there', thus he keeps becoming the doer and the bearer. 'I am' and 'I am the mind' – as long as this notion is alive, the force of the *vāsanās* will keep on giving rise to new desires and thoughts every moment. And in order to fulfil those desires, the *Jiva* keeps on performing new actions every moment.

Thus it keeps getting entangled in the chain reaction of *karma*. For example, a father comes home and takes out all the anger he feels towards his boss, on his unsuspecting wife. The wife is incapable of retaliating but is angry nevertheless and she takes out her anger on the child. The child, in turn, takes out his anger on his school book and rips off its pages – this is chain reaction of *karma*.

Your *karmic* force gave you your current set of parents and their *karmic* force, in turn, made you their child. Now your pain, your suffering is their pain, their suffering and vice versa. 'I and mine' makes you attach your mind to people and objects. And if anything happens to what you regard as yours and are attached to so dearly, you suffer. Say, if you attach your mind to this flower, then when the flower shrivels, you will feel sad. If someone snatches it from you, you will get angry. And if you are very attached to it, then you may well go and get another flower. This is what you do with your relationships, don't you? One relationship breaks off, you form another one. If unhappy with relatives, you bond with friends; if friends turn out to be no good, you make friends with strangers – facebook! Thus the *Jiva* is in great turmoil – pining for pleasure, yearning for happiness, craving for sensory gratification. And in this yearning, it keeps on doing manifold actions but doesn't realise that he will have to bear the fruit of his every action.

As alluded to earlier, the cycle of *karma* is the cycle of time, for *karma* happens in time and one bears fruits in time. Thus one can say that *karma* is time and time is *karma*. As long as the mind is, so are its experiences of pain and pleasure, anger and envy, lust and greed. But when it disappears in the lap of deep sleep, then what desires, what anger, what lust! Even the most ill-tempered man looks like an angelic child when asleep. He is not, but looks so innocent in his sleep. Once a lady came to meet her friend and found her two year old son sleeping blissfully on the couch. 'So cute, he looks like an angel', she cooed. But the mother retorted, 'say that when he is awake, my dear, that is if he doesn't bite off your head first!'

Get this straight – whosoever your mind becomes dependent upon for happiness, in a way, you start hating that person. Look at husbands and wives - they fight, then they make up, then they fight and it goes on like this. The locality I grew up in had a couple who would constantly keep fighting, abusing each other. Verbal abuses, exchanging physical blows, but then, I saw that all this hatred notwithstanding, the lady would bear a child every year like clockwork! I particularly remember seeing her one day with an infant in her arms, four kids tagging along and on top of that she was pregnant with yet another child. She was walking with her troupe whilst verbally abusing her husband! How could she sleep with a man she loathed so much? Height of foolishness and dopiness! Minds are completely incompatible but such is the biological need for physical copulation that they kept on producing child after child. And then finally someone compelled her to undergo sterilisation. Now the way you people are, I think all of you ought to be sterilised! Your progeny will be like you, rather is likely to be lowlier than you. Sri Guru Nanak Dev has said so aptly, "If a woman wants to beget a child, then she should give birth to a devotee, a sage, a braveheart, else why does she bother to bear children? Why doesn't she remain a *bānjh* (barren)? Where is the question of accomplishing something great by giving birth to greedy, lustful offspring whose minds are full of *vāsanās*, all sorts of inane desires? Why should a woman lose her luster for the sake of such a brood?

Mind is influenced by the wheel, the cycle of time. A newborn baby has no interest in sex. All it wants is food and toys. Then as time passes, with the advent of adolescence, sexual hormones are released in his body and all of a sudden he develops a great attraction for the opposite gender. This attraction wasn't there earlier, but with time, it happens. By virtue of time, the changes occurring in his mind and body ensure to keep him running after sensory indulgence. With time, the objects of desire change. And when the person becomes old, he starts feeling hopeless, depressed, body gets diseased and then dies one day. But given the *vāsanās* in his mind, the wheel of time will ensure that he gets born again at some point in time. And once again the game of the nine planets will start anew.

Given the current dormant state of your intellect, it is indeed the planets that are governing your life. Thus nature's forces are working and running your life. After all, did you choose your birth date and place or did birth happen to you? Look at the face, the eyes of any infant, less than a year old. And you will see certain bewilderment, perplexity in the baby's eyes, for it doesn't know where he is, who the people around him are. Then with passage of time, as he keeps on listening to words like 'my son', 'mummy', 'daddy', the innocent child starts regarding them as his parents. And as the clock keeps ticking, he grows up believing that certain things and people belong to him, taking them to be 'mine'. Thus mind keeps getting more and more entangled in the wheel of time, swaying on the swing of duality – sometimes happy, sometimes sad. Then diseases start taking over one's body as well as those of near and dear ones and a day comes when either they die or he dies. Can you stop any of this? Can you prevent diseases from overpowering your body? Can you escape from the hands of the Grim Reaper when he knocks on your door? Everything is being managed by mind i.e. time. Mind is time and time is mind. The sages ask you to search for your mind, to understand your mind, and as you start fathoming your mind, you come to grips with the concept of time. It is indeed a very mysterious game!

Reverting to the nine planets and their influence on your life – the exact time and place of your birth has a deep connection with the planets and their effect. At the time of birth, the combination of the nine forces along with place and time determines the kind of life journey the *Jiva* will go through. All the incidents, events are fixed, pre-determined. When the venerable Jijamata Bai was pregnant with Chatrapati Shivaji, she had asked their family astrologer to predict what sort of a child she would bear. The learned scholar had replied, 'He could become a great man provided his birth takes place at a particular time. If, on the other hand, he gets born before that time, he will neither be good for you nor to himself.'

Now, Jijabai was a very virtuous, a devout religious lady. And she was determined to give birth to a child who would grow up to fight for the freedom of the Marathas. She did not want some sense gratification-pursuing twit. Given her strong resolve for a valiant, gutsy son, it is said that she remained tied up in inverted posture, so as to delay the birth. Labour pains started, but such was her incredible tenacity that she refused to give birth. She endured the labour pains until the right time, only then did she get untied to give birth to Shivaji. The time of first breath that a neonate takes exerts a tremendous influence on his entire life. That is why exact location in longitude and latitude along with the precise time is crucial, very critical indeed. But not every woman can be a Jijabai. It is said that whilst she was enduring the severe labour pains, she continued reciting *mantras*; such a dedicated spiritual practitioner was that noble lady.

It is indeed a lamentable tragedy that today's Indian women have no clue about the astrological science behind the birth of a child. They don't know when they get pregnant and they are totally ignorant of the importance of the time of the baby's birth. As I stated earlier, the *karmic* force of the parents is linked to that of their offspring. Thus, if Jijabai's *karma* was such, then so was Shivaji's. After all, can it be easy for a baby wanting to come out of the womb but being prevented from doing so? This reflects the calibre of the *Jiva* and thus it got the womb of an equivalent calibre along with the matching *karmic* forces.

The place and the time have the most definite bearing on the progeny's life. And you will be amazed to know that even twins are not born at the same time. There is a difference, albeit of a couple of minutes or seconds, even between the births of twins. And these few seconds or minutes make a world of difference to their lives to come. Thus we can say that your fate was already sealed at the moment of your birth. It is hard to accept but this, nevertheless, is the proverbial bitter truth.

Chapter-12

DESTINY OR FREE WILL?

Destiny or free will? This issue always leads to an impassioned debate with clueless folk fervidly defending one over the other. Many people have asked this rather overworked question to me: what is stronger, who wins – fate or free will? Is everything pre-determined, down to your *kismet* or is there any role of free will? The answer lies in this symbolic illustration. A dog tied down by a leash to a tree – how far can it go? Only as far as the length of the leash! The fact that the dog is tied down is his fate, his destiny, his *kismet*. The dog can, however, move around within the distance allowed by the length of the leash. Say, if the leash is ten feet long, then the dog can move around within a distance of ten feet – this is its free will. But it cannot move beyond ten feet. Your mind is that dog which is tied down by the leash of your *kismet*, fate which in turn was decided right at the time of your birth. What you will attain, what you will suffer, all the incidents you will have to face in your life – this is your fate and it is sealed right at the time of your birth.

Imagine a dog being dragged along by its owner, from place

A to place B. On the way, the dog sees a bitch and wants to move towards her but the owner pulls the leash tightly and yanks him in the other direction. The dog struggles and in the bargain hurts his neck. Moreover, as his attention is somewhere else, he misses seeing the ditch ahead and falls into it. The owner hauls the dog out and holding the leash tightly, drags him along. Similarly, all *Jiva* are tied down by the leash of their *karma*, and this *karmic* force is yanking the *Jiva* in a particular direction. That is why it happens that though you don't want to experience many things yet you are forced to do so; you don't want to do something but your *karmic* force propels you to face the consequences of your previous *karma*. In the meanwhile, the dog of your mind is drooling over this object, that object, wanting to be with this relationship, away from that — this pulling and pushing gives you nothing but suffering.

Now, let's say the above mentioned dog becomes wise. Thus now when its owner is tugging it along, the dog doesn't resist. Instead, he obediently follows the master. And dog owners would know that whilst walking a compliant dog, they don't have to hold the leash tightly. Thus the dog reaches the destination along with its owner. And the master, pleased by the dog's compliant, yielding behaviour, lovingly pats it on the back saying, 'good dog'. For the master is assured that the dog is very faithful and obedient, thus he removes the leash from the dog's neck.

An ignorant man's mind is that dog which never becomes wise. He keeps fighting his own *karmic* force, his own *prārabdha*, his own fate. 'Why me', 'why did i get this father', 'why am I not beautiful', 'why am I not intelligent', 'why am I not rich', 'why did I get this disease' – the dog of your mind keeps resisting, keeps fighting with its own destiny. That is why it suffers. He is a sage, a master, a *sādhu* who gives up fighting with his fate. He makes peace with the leash held by time. He wholeheartedly accepts all that is to happen through his body in this lifetime. Be what shall, let thy will be. No resistance, no complaints, no fighting. When the dog of your mind starts walking along with time, then know that God is the master, the Lord of time. So we can say that one whose mind merges with the Lord stops fighting with his fate. And such is the devotion, the love awakened in his mind towards his master that one day, the Lord removes the leash of time from the his neck. This is what is meant by *moksha*, salvation.

But until the dog doesn't become wise, the master will have to drag, have to yank it along and beat it into submission. Your destiny drags you along, beats you into compliance. You fight, you resist, you get angry, you get frustrated – you are simply not willing to accept your destiny, which ironically enough, was created by none other than you, through your past *karma*. You don't want to be accountable for your actions, you don't want to own up to your responsibility but time will not let you escape it. No one could or can escape the mighty clutches of time.

It is said that the Sri Rama had killed Bali on the sly, shooting an arrow at him whilst hiding behind a tree. *Purānās* say that thousands of years later, Rama was born again in the form of Sri Krishna. Several decades later, near the city of Dwarika, a hunter shot a poison-tipped arrow which hit Sri Krishna's foot whilst he was resting under a tree. That became the cause of his body's death in that lifetime. Now, the hunter didn't do this deliberately. He mistook the silhouette under the tree to be a deer and thus aimed at it. The hunter came to find his 'prey' and was stunned to see that his arrow had hit the Lord, Sri Krishna. He fell down on his knees weeping inconsolably at what had happened through his hands. But Sri Krishna comforted him saying, 'no cause for any remorse dear, for the account has now been settled.' In our previous birth, I was Rama and you were Bali. The score is now even. It is time for me to shed this body; moreover, it is the right time for me to bear the fruit of having killed you in your previous lifetime. Thus don't be despondent, don't be remorseful for it is no fault of yours. Be burden-free. Then Sri Krishna entered the state of *samādhi* and merged the *prāna* from his gross body into *mahā prāna*; merged his mind into *Māyā* and what to say about the *Ātman* – it is *Brahman*, neither coming nor going anywhere!

Thus accept this irrefutable fact that your destiny was sealed at the time of your birth. Imagine a man has been trapped, imprisoned in a pitch-dark room and he is aimlessly wandering in the darkness, stumbling and falling. Say he happens to see a narrow beam of light entering the room from the corner of a wall. And focussing on that light beam, he follows it to a small hole in the wall. Then, with full concentration, he starts to make the hole wider, pulling out the brickwork gradually such that the hole becomes wide enough for him to emerge out of the prison.

The *Jiva* trapped in the noose of *karma* needs at least a trace of *punya karma,* which can be likened to the narrow beam of light in the above example. And *Jiva* do get some opportunity to escape the noose when a light beam of knowledge manages to reach. But, if he fails to make the right connection with the source of that light beam i.e. the sage, the master, then the opportunity is lost! And who knows when it will knock on your door again. The sage, the master is spreading the ray of light in the dark prison of your mind. But I re-iterate, in the absence of *punya karma,* a being cannot reach here. He may drop off a relative at the ashram gate and leave. And even if he meets me, he will not have the eyes to recognise who I am. He will just focus on my external appearance, no more than that. And of what use is that? If you do not connect your mind with me, then will the ray of knowledge ever reach you through me? Furthermore, there are folk who because of *pāpa karma* end up harbouring animosity towards me. They disparage, belittle, denigrate – mind you, it doesn't make any difference to me. But as alluded to earlier, if you throw a ball against a wall, it will bounce

Karma Unravelled

back to you. Likewise, if someone slings mud at a sage, then he has to bear the burden of that ignoble act.

Reverting to fate versus free will, I can say that given your present condition it is fate alone playing the entire game. Your will comes into play only when your Sun and Mercury get awakened and robust. But this will not happen until your *karma* are superior and that in turn will not occur until your mind becomes superior. Thus the *Jiva* is tied down by the rope of its *prārabdha*, and indeed it is difficult to untie this rope. Yes, the length of the rope varies. Someone sees me on a television channel and changes the channel — his rope was only that long. Whereas, another fellow, listens to me and comes to the *ashram*! *Punya karma* and free will are interconnected like this: you will do *punya karma* if your intellect is developed well, and your intellect will be ripened through the effect of your *punya karma*! Someone may well come to the *ashram* but is unable to understand my words, that is his fate. And some may well understand my words but not put them into practice, again it is down to his fate.

If certain specific planetary combinations take place at the time of birth, then there will be virtuosity and spiritual ascension in the person's lifetime. Otherwise, nothing of the sort will happen. Thus astrology scriptures say that if someone understands this veritable truth and desperately wants to come out of the vicious cycle of *karma*, then he needs to pray sincerely, seek the company of sages, serve them and take refuge in the guru. The more he stays in the proximity of the guru, the more he purifies his mind through service and the more his intellect and mind will change for the better. When intellect and mind change, so does your *karma*, and as the *kriyāmān karma* change so will the *agāmi karma*. It is all indeed deeply interrelated.

As the intellect gets awakened through *satsang*, service and spiritual practices, virtuous acts will start happening through you which will further uplift you on the spiritual path. Now, this will happen neither because of fate alone nor via free will alone – it will only occur through the combination of the two. And the third factor, which you seldom ponder over, is the grace of a sage, a guru, a master – for it is way, way above both fate and free will. So if all these three factors are working in your favour viz. fate, free will and the guru's grace, then alone can you come out of this otherwise inexorable wheel of *karma*. Else, there is no chance at all, none whatsoever.

Whatsoever *dhrida karma* you have done, you will invariably have to bear the consequences, the fruits of those actions – be it auspicious or inauspicious. Until and unless you don't bear the fruit, the *karmic* force does not get exhausted. Just as missiles fired at a set distance get burnt out only after hitting the target, likewise the missile of your *karma* gets burnt out only after it gives you the fruit of your actions. Not before that! Thus Gurbani says, 'why blame anyone else for the consequences of your own actions? Accept whatever is happening and if you don't want this nonsense to continue then take refuge at the feet of a sage – there is no other way out.'

Astrology texts state that those who were your enemies in your previous birth take on birth as your children in this lifetime, so as to make you suffer by being your progeny. On the other hand, your previous *punya karma* can also beget you such offspring who can become the cause of your liberation.

There is a well known incident from the life of Tulsidas. He was much attached to his beautiful wife and such was his attraction for her that once, out of sheer desperation to be with her, he used a corpse to sail across a flooded river and then climbed up to her room with the aid of a snake that he mistook to be a rope. It is said that the wife condemned his behaviour harshly, saying: 'all this effort for union with a mere body, a bag of muscle and bones? If only you had such devotion for the Lord, you would have well attained Him by now.' And such was the radical effect of her words that at that very instant, Tulsidas's attachment for his wife vanished into thin air. Thus the wife's denunciation turned out to be a blessing for Tulsidas. Similarly, had Prahlad's father (Hiranyakashipu) not been the demon that he was, preventing the son from worshipping Vishnu, perhaps Prahlad would have never become such a staunch devotee of the Lord. The more the father threatened and abused him, the more devout he became. Good and bad from the societal viewpoint are different to that from the spiritual viewpoint.

So, the bottom line is that we have to endure the fruits of our *dhrida* (unalterable) *karma*. As far as *dhrida-adhrida* type of *karma* is concerned, it means there is some possibility of alteration, provided there is concentrated effort on your part. If one works really hard, sincerely and perseveringly, then some alteration can be brought about in this category of *karma*. *Adhrida karma*, on the other hand, can be altered through effort and grace of a master. See, simple cough and cold can be easily treated through potions and home-made remedies. But what can anyone do about inherited genetic diseases? Is there any potion for mentally retarded children? Many a time parents of such children ask me if it was due to their *karma* that they begot such children? Well, it is not only their *karma* but the *karma* of the child too – it is their combined *karma* which has put them in such a relationship. But don't ever jeer or deride anyone for their physical or mental disabilities. If you can't be compassionate then at least be fearful of your own *karma phala* which may spring up anytime, for you don't know which fruit will crop up without giving you any warning.

Kabir Sahib says: 'O Mind! How can I mend your ways? You have defeated me. How much and how long have you made me ramble in this labyrinthine world? At least now let go of me, let me be free.' Kabir Sahib further says, 'I begged and I beseeched but the mind did not relent. Then I met my guru, and he chopped the rope of my bondage. He killed my mind. Now, the mind is no more.'

Guru saves you from the noose of your mind. But remember, he does not perform any miracle. You have to put in the effort of consistent, determined spiritual practise. But there again comes the issue of fate versus will! How long is your leash, only that much will you be able to do! What's more, if your wretched mind does not get the grace of a sage and it is not prayerful, then nothing can be done. Then, there is no escape. On a positive note, although change is very difficult, it is not impossible. So, there is hope for everyone provided you make sincere effort, be prayerful and take refuge at the feet of an enlightened master.

Chapter-13

ASTROLOGY: THE NITTY GRITTY

By now you must have grasped the importance of the vital role of astrology in every aspect of life; linking past, present and future with the thread of *karma* principle. Let's now delve deeper into the ins and outs of this science. As detailed earlier, the precise time of birth and location (in longitude and latitude) reveal the planetary conditions at that moment, in that location, which has a strong bearing on the fate of the individual. Not only that but by reading the chart one can have an overall idea of the physical, emotional and mental characteristics of the person – his education, wealth, family life, health and so on. An astute astrologer can foretell how a newborn baby would look like when he or she grows into adult hood – the physical attributes, facial features, body shape, skin colour, hair texture and so on! The basic astrological chart is divided into twelve houses, each described in a nutshell as follows:

ভ The first house describes the overall character, the overall personality of the individual, including physical features and health.

ভ Second house pertains to speech, family and wealth. How much wealth one will have, what will be one's style, manner of speech and what sort of family one will have.

৪ Third house tells about the person's hobbies, siblings as to the number and nature of his brothers and sisters; whether he will be the youngest or the oldest or the middle sibling. It reveals how brave, courageous and powerful the individual will be.

৪ Fourth house pertains to the individual's home, his family life, and his nurturing values. You may be amazed to know that an adroit astrologer can even tell you the colour of your walls, whether there is any school, temple, or garden near your house, how big is the house, what is at the front of the house, what is at the backside, what is on the sides, whether the person will own the house or rent it, how many houses will he possess and the like. It is after all a science and never errs in its predictions. Also, the fourth house reveals how much happiness the person will get from his family life.

৪ Fifth house discloses mental inclinations, intelligence and mantra siddhi. If there is any powerful, any auspicious planet in this house, it has a strong bearing on the spiritual ascension of that individual. It reveals what sort of spiritual practice the person will do, and if he will attain any mantra siddhi in this lifetime. Moreover, it reveals the person's intelligence quotient both in the material world and in the realm of dharma, spirituality. That is why though children are born to the same parents, looked after equally well and taught by same teachers, yet their achievement levels vary. This is revealed by the status of the fifth house. One can also know about the fellow's mental inclination i.e. which topics and subjects will he be interested in.

৪ Sixth house describes disease, debt, enemies and struggle in the person's life – what sort of diseases, how many diseases; how much debt if any; how many enemies; how much struggle will he have to face in his life. If this house is strong, the person will be competitive and always win over his enemies. If it is weak, then the person will always be afflicted by some or the other disease, will face some enemy or the other, and keep on paying some debt or the other.

പ Seventh house pertains to marriage, spouse, business partners and public acclaim. It indicates how will the person's marriage be and how many times he will get married. Many a time one sees that a marriage that has been fixed, gets broken for some reason or the other; sometimes right at the time of the ceremony. This is not accidental! The seventh house reveals the nature of the spouse and whether the person will have a happy or stressful married life. Also, it shows the nature of business partners i.e. whether they will be honest or deceitful, helpful or of the hindering kind and so on.

പ Eighth house pertains to tapa as well as research, mysterious, and unethical activities. It shows if the person will be inclined towards occult sciences, research, and especially if he will carry out any yogic practice. I may well shout from the rooftop asking everyone to do āsanās but if the planets are not conducive, you will not do them or will not be interested in them at all. Now, this house also talks about some mysterious things, which may be good or bad. For example, whether the person will be interested in inner evolution, mantra and tantra, whether he will perform austere practices or not. I have seen that sages and masters tend to have a very strong eighth house. And the indicators are very clear such that the person would have become a sage no matter where he would have been born – in India or abroad. So the eighth house strongly relates to spiritual ascension. But then, it also refers to some unethical activities. Although having said that, worldly folk regard the life of a sannyāsi (renunciate) as unethical! That is why, especially in olden times, people would refrain from inviting renunciates to marriage ceremonies. After all, would a renunciate give blessings for more worldly entanglement or otherwise?!

പ Ninth house refers to dharma, destiny and punya. It is also regarded as the father's house. If this house is strong, then the person will invariably progress on the path of dharma. In addition, if his fifth house is strong too, he will attain mantra siddhi and if along with these two, the eighth house is also strong then the person becomes a great seeker, a great performer of austerities. Ninth house also reveals the fate with respect to material gains, family life, education, wealth, marital life and children. It also reveals how much punya one has accrued. Insights about your previous life are seen from the characteristics of your ninth house. Now, if someone had accrued a lot of punya in his previous lifetime, then the ninth house will have Bṛhaspati and the Sun.

ॐ Tenth house refers to karma, profession & employer. Whether the person will be inclined to work or be an idle, good for nothing fellow, whether he will be a workaholic or work shy, what sort of profession he will have – job or business, and whether he will be an employee or will employ others.

ॐ Eleventh house pertains to profit, gains, rewards, achievements - whether one will gain material things, whether one will attain fame or reach up to some high post or not.

ॐ Twelfth house refers to moksha and also confinement. Now, this confinement can be voluntary (a sage sitting in some isolated cave) or imposed (imprisonment for some crime). It also points to hospitalisation and foreign travel.

See, this is a very broad description. Many parameters are studied with respect to each house, thus the overall analysis is very intricate. But because the aim of this discourse is not to teach you astrology, I am giving a generic overview of the astrological chart and its houses. This should make it clear that nothing is happening as an accident in your life! The houses cover all aspects of your life, not even one is excluded. Thus if the planetary conditions are not good, then the person keeps on suffering – no money, no acclaim, loads of debt, no dearth of enemies, disease upon disease, no spiritual evolution. And because of the pain and suffering, people keep thronging outside temples, gurudwaras. Such long queues! This is not because they are devoted to the Lord, No Sir! They seek the deity's *darshan* in the hope that the said deity will eradicate their pain, their miseries and bestow good fortune upon them. But if you solemnly ponder over this you will realise that if this is the way everyone's suffering gets wiped out, then will it not disprove the law of *karma*? The sages who shed light upon the principle of *karma*, will they and their knowledge not be deemed wrong? Will it not make Sri Krishna a liar and prove the Gita be a big fat lie, a deception?

Every seed carries the potential of growing into a tree. But it will take time for the tree to manifest from a seed – it could be several years before a seed transforms into a fully grown tree. Likewise, these twelve houses of the astrological chart; at the time of your birth, you bring them along in the form of seeds. But the pages of the book of your life get revealed gradually in due course of time. The science of astrology is very amazing, very amazing indeed. It tells you how much *punya* and *pāpa* you have brought along with you. And this will naturally affect the kind of life you will have. Moreover, remember, you were born because of your own *karmic* force. No one compelled you to take birth. Everything in your life is related to your previous *karma* – including the shape, height and appearance of your body. Thus you cannot blame God for how you look, what you have or don't have in your life, how your parents are, how your siblings are, how your spouse is, for everything is down to your own *karma*.

Our ancient sages didn't have to make or look at anyone's astrological chart to assess them. Just one look at the individual and the sage would know his entire past, his present and what potential he held for the future. And if they saw that there was no possibility of any spiritual growth, they would refuse to accept that person as their disciple – no matter how much the fellow would implore. It would be made very clear to the person that the time for spiritual upliftment had not yet come. They wouldn't give even a single precept to that person because they knew the person would never follow it. Yet they wouldn't dishearten people either and hence tell them to do pilgrimage, serve their parents and do virtuous acts. But no more than that! In contrast, modern times are indeed strange. Any person can access esoteric knowledge through the internet, videos, CDs. But this wasn't the case in ancient times. Then, a disciple could get to listen to lofty words of wisdom only from the guru, who would decide when to impart the knowledge. It would be imparted only to a capable person who had the capacity to imbibe it.

Note that even the planets have what is known as a *dashā*. For example, on a cloudless day, the sun sparkles radiantly in the sky. But if it becomes very cloudy or stormy then the sun gets concealed and the morning feels like evening time. Thus even if say the ninth house has all the auspicious planets but if they are weak, powerless, then it is of no use. And they are weak because the person's *punya* from his previous lifetime is sparse. It is the quantum of your *punya* that brings happiness, knowledge and *dharma* in your life. Now, you may be surprised to know but your past life's *vāni* i.e. speech has a bearing on your current life's *karma* and profession. Thus be careful of what you speak, how you speak because it is shaping your future. Speech comes from the mind. But does this mean that if the mind is *sattvaguni* so shall be your speech, and if your mind is *rajoguni* so will be your speech? No, things are not so straightforward either. The mind may well be *sattvaguni* but if a wave of *rajoguna* arises at the time of speaking – the speech will but naturally be *rajoguni*. Likewise, the mind may well be *rajoguni* but if a *tamoguni* wave arises – how will the speech be?

Tamoguni, abusive, offensive. Your speech reflects your thoughts, your emotions and your intellect.

Your quantum of *punya* accrued from previous lifetime is evident from the ninth house, and the tenth house reveals your *karma* in your current life. Not only this, but the tenth house also indicates *karma* done in the previous lifetime. And the sixth house reveals the previous *pāpa karma* which lead to diseases in this life. If these are *dhrida*, then there will be no treatment for the ailment; if *adhrida* it will be curable, and in the case of *dhrida-adhrida*, health of such an individual will be up and down. *Pāpa* means pain, suffering and what are diseases if not pain, suffering?

All the houses are interconnected. If the ninth house is powerless, then that affects the sixth house which relates to *pāpa* related illnesses. The ninth house also influences your second house. Thus, what sort of people are there in your family is related to your previous *karma*. If quantum of *pāpa* is excessive, then the enemies from your previous life will become your kith and kin in this lifetime – your siblings, mother, father, or children. Nothing is accidental or incidental.

Srimad Bhāgwat narrates a story of a king who did not have any children despite having several queens. With utmost hope in his mind, he married yet again and this time round his wife begot a son. The king's joy knew no bounds. He was over the moon with happiness, and he raised his son with a lot of love and affection. But this made the other queens very cross and then, one day, out of jealousy, they poisoned the prince and he died. The shell-shocked king could not bear the departure of his beloved son. He wept inconsolably, beseeching the deities to help him. It is said that sage Nārad appeared before him and tried to console the disconsolate king. The sage said, 'Stop weeping O king. Who do you shed tears for? That *Jiva* is gone.' The king, however, wouldn't listen and appealed for his son to be brought back to life. The sage replied,

'But he wouldn't want to do so.' The king insisted, 'You call upon his soul and I will talk to him.' The sage relented and the *Jiva* appeared in front of the king. The king wailed, 'O beloved son, please come back to life. Tell me who killed you and I will avenge your death.' The *Jiva* replied, 'What son, whose son? I have no affection for you. In my previous lifetime, you were my sworn enemy who had harmed me a lot. I waited a long time to be born to your wife so that I could take my revenge upon you. And seeing you in such a state of distress, I have accomplished what I wanted to. As far as avenging my death is concerned, it has nothing to do with you. By killing me, the queens have got even with me, for I had harmed them in my previous birth. Thus now, with all scores settled, why would I want to come back to life as your son?'

You don't get tired repeating 'she is mine', 'he is mine', but in reality, who is yours? No one! It is your previous *karma* which make someone your father, someone your mother, someone your child. These relationships are nothing but a settlement of the *punya* and *pāpa karma* connected to them. Your past and present are deeply connected, interrelated. Take example of a mother who has three children but one child is most endeared to her, the other is lesser loved and she has neutral feelings for the third child. Why? Again, because of previous *karmic* account!

The fourth house is the eighth when you start counting from the ninth house. The eighth house, as stated earlier, is related to your previous austerities, and also unethical activities. Your previous *tapa* affects what sort of a mother you will have in this life, and what sort of relationship you will have with her. So, today's happiness is determined by past life *tapa* and today's suffering is because of previous life's unethical, sinful activities.

The third house is the seventh from the ninth house. When you start counting from the ninth house, the seventh becomes the third house. This indicates that your present materialistic desires, your present hobbies, interests too are not incidental. There is a reason why someone likes reading, whilst someone else is interested in music and so on. Your past life's desires become your present life hobbies, interests. Thus your likes, your tastes, your proclivities are all linked to your past desires. Some children want to play with toys all the time with no interest in reading or eating. Whilst others may just want to eat all the time and some others may want to be outdoors all the time. They are expressing their desires, their tastes from their previous lifetimes. Incidentally, I know of a five year old child who is neither interested in toys, games, books or food. When asked what he would like to become when he grows up, he promptly answers, 'I want to become a monk, a *sādhu*!' Now, who must have taught him that?! His parents have no such disposition. He has brought his interests along with him.

In a nutshell, you are responsible for your actions and their consequences. Whatsoever be your present situation, know that it is only because of your own previous *karma* and nothing else. And your present *karma* will become the causative factor of your future situations. Thus live wisely. What this also entails is that accept your past as it was. You cannot change your past. Thus, rather than fretting over why something happened or didn't happen in your past, it is wise to live your present with wisdom and awareness. Your present should be your only concern, neither your past nor your future.

Chapter-14

TAKE THE EXIT

Get this clear that all the astrology I have elucidated to you is in context of the principle of *karma*. And secondly, as an eye-opener, so that you realise the futility of desires! It is your past desires which are the cause of your present suffering, and thus wisdom lies in not giving rise to newer and newer desires. Don't fall again and again in the trench of desires; steady yourself once and for all. And extricate your mind from the rat race of desires and engage it in doing *punya karma*. It does not matter if you did or didn't do any spiritual practise in the past, but rather whether you do any in your present is what matters. Maybe your planets are not conducive for attainment of *mantra siddhi,* but chanting *mantra* in the present is in your hands. So don't worry about how much *punya* or *pāpa* you have done in the past. Focus on your present.

In this context, many people ask me about getting past-life regression done so that they can understand their present better. Why go so far, I say? The way you are entangled in the web of desires and attachment now, something similar must have happened in the past. Moreover, you don't have the strength and endurance to see your past and accept it fully. So, see your present and ensure that your present is bereft of attachment, laziness and any vile or sinful *karma*.

As explained earlier, I re-iterate that you can annihilate the sum total *karma*, the *sanchit karma* but it needs diligent practice of *ashtānga yoga* – *yama, niyama, āsana, prānāyama, pratyāhāra, dhāranā, dhyāna* and *samādhi*. It is possible only if one embarks on this journey, else the vicious loop will continue relentlessly – your past influencing your present, your present influencing your future and so on and on and on. Thus awaken to this reality, and with an inspired enthusiasm, focus upon learning how to become *nishkāma*; learn how to rid the mind of *vāsanās*, how to steady the sense horses, how to tighten the reins of the mind, and how to awaken the sleeping intellect which has been made unconscious by ignorance.

In this context I relate an incident relating to Ramayana. Once Laxman asked his guru, the revered sage Vashishtha, 'O omniscient Gurudev! You know all aspects of time, the past, present and future. You would have most certainly known the fate of Sri Rama after he was taken by sage Vishwamitra to slay demons. You would have known all that was to follow i.e. him marrying Sita, Kaikayi wickedly ensuring Rama's exile, then Rama fighting Ravana and bringing Sita back to Ayodhya only to abandon her for the sake of his subjects.' To this, sage Vashishtha replied, 'let alone I, even your father king Dashratha was well aware of the events to unfold.' This perplexed Laxman even more. 'My own father knew all this and yet he had got so desperately distraught at the moment of Rama's exile that he succumbed to the intense pain of separation? That does not make sense Gurudev', Laxman urged the sage to explain further. Vashishtha replied, 'Laxman, even if man comes to know of his future but if his *chitta* is still shrouded by the cloud of ignorance, then no matter what, his powerless intellect cannot prevent the downfall of his mind. That is why even though King Dashratha was well aware of events to come, when the time came of Rama's departure, his mind broke down into a pool of distress and agony. To the point that despite knowing nothing could be done to prevent the sequence of events to come, he just could not accept the situation and the distraught king succumbed to the intense grief.' Thus if King Dashratha, who was none other than Sri Rama's father and had the grace of the exalted sage Vashishtha, if he could not appropriately cope with the knowledge of the future, do you people have any chance?! Thence don't keep wasting your time by fretting over getting to know your future. The past is past and the future is yet to come, thus don't worry about either. Just focus all your attention on living your present with equanimity and discipline; fill your present with spiritual practices. And you now know very well that these *kriyamān karma* will influence your future. So if you can make a resolve to change your present in this way, then you can certainly create a new future.

Yes, you are bearing the consequences of your previous *karma* in the form of your *prārabdha*, but at the same time note that your present is also very powerful, provided you know how to make the most of it. It is thus entirely up to you how you use your time, whether you put it to good use or end up whiling it away. Live your life wisely, with utmost wisdom. He is wise who, seeing the objective world-inflicted suffering in the future, makes his mind step back from the material world right now itself. What is the source of pain, suffering? You may remember the Gita verse explicated in an earlier chapter: contemplation upon the world of objects and people gives rise to attachment and desire for the said object. If this desire is fulfilled, it leads to greed, and if not it leads to eruptive anger which destroys the intellect. And what will be left in a person's life when his intellect has been destroyed?!

Astrology clearly shows the link between your past and present.

And it is entirely up to you how you spend your present. And mind you, present does not mean this day, this hour or this minute, but rather it refers to this very second. That is how fleeting time is. Every passing second becomes your past. So, if you procrastinate and say 'I will do meditation tomorrow, I will do *kirtan* tomorrow, I will do *āsanās* tomorrow. For now, I would rather eat something, or sleep for a while or do some work' - if you continue with this lifestyle and attitude then your fate will be no different to the dog tied down by a leash. You will keep swinging up and down as per the game played by your planets. If favourable, wealth will be in abundance, and when the planetary situation becomes unfavourable, all the wealth will go as quickly as it came. Likewise, as long as planets are in your favour, children will be obedient but no sooner will the planets change their tune, so will your children – the most obedient child ends up beating the father for his property. How and why did this happen, the father wails!

I say this to you: Don't be afraid of anyone. But yes, be very afraid of your own mind. What sort of thoughts it thinks, what sort of desires it entertains – be very alert to all that is happening in your mind. Say if you find a snake in your house, what will you do? Will you not want to get it out? Or will you happily roam around in the house oblivious of the poisonous snake? Having said that, what harm will the external snake do? Maybe bite you and give you some local pain or at worst, kill your body. But, what about the thousands of snakes of desires that are gripping your mind, for aeons? So many of your lives have they destroyed and yet you continue to live with the slithering snakes of *vāsanās*? How, and why? Search, look for them and uproot them completely.

Refresh your memory with the hierarchical algorithm: *samskārās→vāsanās→desires→sankalpa→karma*. It still takes some time to say this but *karma* happen even quicker than that! So fast, that only after the action has taken place, do you realise that the said *karma* has occurred. 'I didn't realise how that action happened through me' – you keep repeating this statement often. But you will have to keep an eye on your mind. The poisonous crop of desires and thoughts is indeed very lethal. This has to be destroyed, uprooted completely, and this is what the entire journey of spiritual practices (*sādhanā*) involves. No spiritual upliftment is possible in the presence of worldly desires.

There is a very interesting and far-reaching incident from the life of the great *yogi*, Lahiri Mahasaya. It is said that once he was roaming across the Himalayan ranges, searching for his guru, his master. After a great deal of walking, he met a man who said, 'You are looking for our master, the great *yogi*, isn't it? I have come to take you to him but before that you need to bathe in that river first.' So Lahiri Mahasaya took a dip in the river but the instant he did so, the river and the river bed had disappeared and instead he found he was lying on a luxurious bed in what appeared to be a very grand palace. He was surrounded by scores of maids and servants. Some fetched him opulent clothes, others were serving up a lavish, sumptuous meal. Another servant came with a jewel-embedded crown and placed it on Lahiri Mahasaya's head. And then came along a very beautiful woman and a thought arose in his mind 'she is my wife'. Thus he spent a long time enjoying the lavish surroundings, all the opulence and grand comforts, and then fell asleep.

But when he woke up, lo and behold, he found that he was lying on the river bed – the palace had vanished! And the man, who had earlier met him, came along saying, 'now you are ready to meet our master'. O yes! I had come to meet my beloved master, remembered a bewildered Lahiri. He was then taken to a cave wherein sat the most radiant, the most serene faced *yogi* with large lustrous eyes. Lahiri Mahasaya fell down at his feet, earnestly saluting him, tears of happiness brimming in his eyes. The *Maha yogi* said, 'Lahiri, now you are finally ready to meet me. There was this one desire lurking in the recesses of your mind, the desire to live the life of a king. I have got that fulfilled for you. Now that your mind is expunged of desires, I can give you the next precept on the spiritual path.'

How long does the realm of dreams appear? There is no intellect there to assess the sense of time and hence it feels as though so much time has lapsed. But whilst you are dreaming, do you ever doubt the genuinity of the dream-world? It all seems so very real. And remember, your dreams are also based on your desires. Thus more the number of desires, more are the number of dreams. Thence, pontificate upon your dreams. And those who say that they don't get any dreams – well, all this indicates is the deep level of their unconsciousness. So unconscious are they, that they cannot even recollect their dreams!

If you remain entangled in the web of *vāsanās* and desires, then the cycle of *karma*, the cycle of time will continue for you, eternally. Sometimes you will pain others, at other times they will pay you back in kind; sometimes you will make someone happy and at other times they will return happiness to you – this mutual give and take will go on and on. Every life comprises childhood, adulthood, old age and death. And if the quantum of *pāpa karma* is very high, then the baby dies soon after birth. Imagine – first having to face the pain of birth and then death soon after all that suffering. After all, is the process of birth easy for the baby? Lying in a confined space for nine months, the womb, can it be easy? Some *Purānās* liken a mother's womb to hell – the amniotic fluid which the foetus floats in, it urinates in that fluid and then drinks that very fluid. This can be easily seen through 3D ultrasound machines. *Purānās* say a mother's womb is as infernal, as suffocating as hell and the foetus prays to God to free it from the hellish surroundings. It prays that it will do anything so as to never land up in the confined space of a womb again. Then the baby gets born in a state of unconsciousness. And as soon as it develops some awareness, he is brainwashed by the parents into raising newer and newer desires.

Purānas say to the child, 'You have forgotten the promise you gave to God whilst you were suffering in the womb, haven't you? You have got so attached to the parents, siblings of your physical body but you have forgotten He whom you should have been attached to.' Thus your *karma* account keeps growing. And every seed will grow into a tree leading to manifold fruits – *dhrida, adhrida* and *dhrida/adhrida*.

You will be stuck in this vicious loop. He alone, can emerge from this loop, who sincerely wakes up to the resolve of wanting to come out of the bondage of *karma*. *Vairagya* is the second attribute needed, equanimity in life is the third and regular practice is the fourth. Lead a balanced life whilst fulfilling your obligatory duties, knowing that the relationships you have acquired in this life are a consequence of your own *karma*. But now, I have to free my mind of all attachments thus I will carry out my duties towards them but I will never open the account of desires, attachments, again – this should be your resolve.

Sri Krishna says, 'He who empties his mind of all attachments and desires, in such a being's life, *karma* too becomes a mere reflex action, where there is no sense of doership anymore. And if this is not the case, then *karma* will bind, and how strongly they do! But just by listening to my words, you cannot have the attitude of being the non-doer. Listening is merely a beginning. So, how can you live with the attitude of being the non-doer? Through the experiential resolve: 'I am not the body and the body is not mine'. And this is possible through regular practice of *prānāyama, dhyāna* and *yoga-nidra*. But know that you are a novice, a beginner. Hence all these practices will help you first to get your mind quietened from the thunderous roar of the external world. Only then will you really evolve spiritually. All said and done, I often see that despite listening to my words, most people are all the times worried about things and people. 'He did not invite me', 'she did not respect me...' – what sheer nonsense! What will you achieve even if the entire world were to fall at your feet?! Thus get your mind out of the swamp of attachment-aversion. But such is the state of your so-badly trained mind that not only do you play the game of attachment /aversion in your homes but you carry on with that here too, in the ashram. You develop liking for those who act as per your wishes and vice versa. My dears! Don't be so featherbrained. Already you have wasted so much of your time in these absurd, inane charades, and you want to continue with that here, in the ashram, too? Extricate your mind from all such relationships, all this stupid politics.

Just by repeating 'I am the non-doer' you don't become a non-doer. Just by repetitiously saying 'I am the detached witness', you won't become one. It is only by actually experiencing your distinction from the body that your attachment cord with the body gets cut, not before that. Your focus thus, has to be very clear. Ensure that the mind is not enslaved to any sensory object, that the mind is not bound to anything, that the mind is turned inwards. This flame of *vairagya* needs to blaze continually. 'No one other than God is mine, hence I am not interested in getting attached to anyone' – that should be your attitude. I am thus neither interested in making anyone my friend nor my foe. As long as this attitude, this way of thinking doesn't take root in your life, then just by repeating 'I am the non-doer', you ain't becoming one.

It has already been explained that *nishkāma karma* is possible only for a person who has destroyed his ego. 'I and mine' – this has to go. And the resolve should be, 'I am not the body, the body is not mine; I am not the mind, the mind is not mine; I am not the intellect, the intellect is not mine.' Sri Krishna says: You have the choice to perform actions. And how you perform those actions is also up to you. But, says the Lord, you cannot dictate the fruits of those actions – it is not in your hands. Hence don't perform actions for the occurrence of any desired result. Furthermore, the Lord adds that don't think on the lines of why should I perform any action if I am not going to receive the desired fruit of the action? This too is inappropriate. Just perform your duties without any expectation of appreciation and without any desire for the fruit – neither gross nor subtle.

The Lord clearly states to Arjuna: Forgo all attachment to the results of your actions. Don't think about whether an action will result in success or failure, for this too is an attachment to the action, the *karma*. Failure or success should not stop you from doing your duty, your *karma*. Do all actions without analysis of its likely fruit. But the way things are with you, a very common grievance is – I did so much for the other person but what did I get in return? Or, I will do such-and-such thing for you, provided you remember this and return the favour later! Drop this attitude, my dears. Feel compassionate towards those who are in pain and trouble, help them in whichever way you can, without thinking about what you will or won't get in return. Do the needful without any desire for the fruit. Now, some may think it is best not to do any *karma* at all. Well, it is simply not possible. Sri Krishna says that no person can stay without doing actions even for a moment, irrespective of whether he is a worldly person or a renunciate. Thus get it clear that the term '*karma sannyāsa*' doesn't mean renunciation of *karma* or not performing any action. A *karma sannyāsi* 'performs' actions, yet he is not the doer of the actions. For the one whose 'I' is not linked to the mind or intellect doesn't perform actions, rather actions happen through him.

Whatsoever actions that happen through the body, senses or the mind – removing the sense of doer-ship from these is known as *karma sannyāsa*. I am not the body, I am not the senses, I am not the mind and I am not the intellect. Mind thinks and through the senses of perception and action, the thought process gets translated into actions via the physical body. And *karma sannyāsa* involves seeing oneself as a distinct witness of the activities of the mind, intellect, senses and body; knowing that I am neither the doer of the actions nor the bearer of their consequence. I am just the detached witness of all the activities of the mind, intellect, senses and body. I neither motivate nor incite any action. I am neither the creator of actions nor am I the bearer of their fruits – auspicious or inauspicious. But this can happen only when I see myself as being separate from the body, senses, mind and intellect – only then can one become a *karma sannyāsi*.

Sri Krishna says, both *karma sannyāsa and nishkāma karma yoga* lead to your supreme welfare but between the two, *nishkāma karma* is superior because it is relatively easier to follow. Now, how is it simpler, you may ask? Herein comes the concept of devotion, *bhakti*. The *bhakta*, the devotee says, 'this body, this mind and this intellect belongs to you O Lord! Thus all actions, all *karma* also belong to the Lord.' 'I am nobody', says the devotee. And as everything belongs to the Lord, the *bhakta* says, 'O God! You operate this intellect, you beget thoughts in this mind, I know only one thing i.e. I am yours and you are mine.' A devotee is blissfully absorbed in utmost devotion unto the divine and has nothing to do other than devoting himself to the Lord. He has no other desire, no other want.

The devotee sees the Lord in all forms, in all beings. Thus he has no enemies for he sees his beloved Lord in one and all. And *nishkāma karma* is easy for the one who has such sincere sentiments of devotion. See, when the body-mind-intellect is mine, the *karma* too is mine. But when these are not mine, then how can the *karma* be mine? A devotee empties himself of everything. He says, 'I am nobody, whatever is, is you O Lord! This 'I', howsoever it is, is not separate from you. Thus O Lord! Whatsoever you get done through this 'I' is good for me and whatsoever that you give is good for me – be it happiness or suffering, acclaim or condemnation, profit or loss. Whatsoever you give is *prasād* for me and I accept this sweet blessing with gratitude' – this is *nishkāma karma yoga*. *Karma* intended for the Lord and offered unto the Lord is *nishkāma karma*. Who am I? Nothing. Everything and everyone belongs to the Lord. I am nothing and nothing belongs to me, inclusive of this body, mind and intellect. Thus everything is happening as per the divine will. O Lord! You are the *karma* and the doer of the *karma*, you are the benefactor and the benefaction too, is you.

With *karma sannyāsa* comes the path of *gyāna yoga*. *Gyāna yoga* involves becoming decisively clear about what the body is, what the mind is, what the intellect is, and then getting firsthand experience of this knowledge – the one with such stillness, such focus, such contemplation can enter the realm of *karma sannyāsa*. But in comparison, it is easier to enter *nishkāma karma yoga* by following the path of love and devotion. All said and done, the basic point is that if your intellect keeps getting stuck in the swamp of attachments, how will you be able to follow any path, be it *nishkāma karma* or path of knowledge or indeed any other path of liberation? Thus if you are seriously and sincerely looking for an exit from the vice-like grip of ignorance, if you are resolutely determined to step down from the inexorable wheel of *karma*, from the ruthless cycle of time then you need to clear all fog of doubt from your mind and bring it single-pointedly on the track of *sādhanā*.

So the first task is to get your mind out of the swamp it is stuck in, which is possible only in the presence of *vairagya* (dispassion). Thence said Sri Krishna to Arjuna: Listen to what I am saying, for only by listening will the fire of dispassion blaze in your heart and raze all your attachments. And the eradication of all attachments will purify your intellect. Keep your mind calm, equanimous, free of duality, free of desires. Do your duties without expectations and deal with your relations only to the extent needed without getting entangled in the web of attachment/aversion. If you have to face tough situations, then so be it. See it as a settlement of your own *karma*.

This is so very well put by Kabir Sahib, 'Nothing to take and nothing to give, I am perpetually immersed in the realm of inner joy.' Thus don't keep beating the old drum, 'she didn't acknowledge me, he didn't respect me...!' Be expectation-less. And when the mind feels low or sad for whatever reason, at that time join your mind to the Lord, to a *mantra*, to the guru. However, in context of the guru, people often make the mistake of having expectations from even the guru – again the same old foolishness! At home expect the parents, the children to appreciate and respect you, and in the ashram expect the guru to do the same?!

How should be your relationship with your guru? Just like the *chakor's* (a bird) relationship with the moon. From afar it keeps on lovingly calling out to the moon. Does the moon ever reply back? Such should be the love for the master, without any expectation, without any desire. Otherwise these desires will also give you pain. When you start working upon making your mind desire-free, expectation-free, the fact is that then you don't have to ask for joy. Then the shower of joy continually falls on the plane of your mind. Your desires have enslaved you. The day you become free of this enslavement, you yourself will become the master. Thus don't lose to your mind, don't fight your mind, but rather understand your mind – the wretched thing is pining for its source. Thus take it close to its source and all its agitations will end instantaneously.

Even the most ignorant man in this world experiences peace in deep sleep. Now why is this so? This is because then the mind is very close to its origin, its source. But because of the veil of ignorance it cannot experience its joyful presence. In meditation, with awareness one goes close to that very root, experiences sheer bliss and then becomes ever-satiated. Then the mind runs nowhere, for having attained the blissful name of the Lord, it is in a state of complete repose. No longer does it want anything. No more yearning, no more searching, no more desires – such is the state of peace, joy and repose. Such a hallowed being experiences the bliss of *moksha* whilst being in the body, whilst being alive. Such a man of realisation is not ruffled by anything. If times are adverse, so be it. He doesn't lament, he doesn't complain. If wealth goes away, the world will declare him as a pauper but the sage says, 'I left the wealth long ago!' An ordinary ignorant person, on the other hand, will weep and wail over the loss of objects and relationships. Moreover, for a sage, there is nothing auspicious or inauspicious. Whatsoever is happening, is happening for the good – this is his attitude, for he is free of all duality.

When Sri Ramakrishna's body developed cancer in the throat region, Narendra (earlier name of Swami Vivekananda) would fight with him saying, 'why don't you cure yourself?' Ramakrishna would calmly reply, 'when I am not unwell, where is the question of becoming well then?' Narendra would insist, 'please cure the cancer in your throat', and the master would laugh it off saying, 'ask the throat to do so, why are you bothering me?!' 'But it is your throat', Narendra would protest. And the master would smile back saying, 'let alone the throat, this entire body is not mine. My dear boy! Neither am I this body and nor are you that body. So forget this argument and let's talk about something else.'

Sages are indeed so amazing! One such sage whom I went to see was having a high fever and was lying all wrapped up in a blanket. On asking what had happened, he coolly replied, 'nothing, this wretched body must have done something in the past and hence has to bear the fruit. Let the rascal bear it. How are you anyway? What would you like to eat?!' On the other hand, what is your attitude to your body's illness?! Trivial complaint or serious disease, you cry all the time. Another sage acquaintance became quite ill in her old age and had to be hospitalised. When I went to see her, she was so happy to see me that she tried to sit up despite all the drips in her arms. She welcomed me with a beaming smile and when asked how she was, she replied, 'I am having a great time. All these educated doctors and nurses keep running around me. I am enjoying all the attention!'

When the entire life seems no more than a play, a game, what to say about diseases? A sage regards them too as just another act of the drama. No aversion, no attachment, no desires, no expectations! And this life is meant for achieving this state of being. It wasn't meant for running after this ever-changing world of objects and people. This entire game of *Māyā* around you exists so that you manage to emerge out of it. But alas! Such is the deep rooted ignorance that people don't want even to understand it, let alone follow this path of liberation.

This then is the realm of *karma*, a very profound, intricately complex topic that needs a lot of investigation, a lot of contemplation. I would suggest that for this deeper understanding, refer to my discourses on the Bhagavad Gita – listen and reflect upon my words. Along with this follow the guidelines I have cited earlier viz. regular practice of *āsana, prānāyama, mantra sādhanā* and so on. That is if you want to change your life for the better! Or do you want to be like the fellow who wrote yesterday, 'my previous *karma* are good and so is my present and I am not interested in *moksha* anyway, what do you have to say to me?' Well, what can I say to a pig happily eating filth?! Carry on eating! Whether to be perpetually trapped in the bondage of *karma* by being the doer or whether to make efforts in emerging out of this trap? The choice is yours. And if you do want to be the non-doer then you have to know your real identity which is distinct from the body, senses, mind and intellect. But this will require sincere effort on your part. Free will or fate, who will win?!!!

On a positive note, irrespective of whether your intellect has grasped the meaning of my words, one thing is for sure that the words have made some imprint on your mind. Now whether you evolve in this very lifetime or not, the *samskārās* cannot be erased by time. A moment will come when like a flash of lightening you will grasp the meaning in your core and shout aloud an Archimedean 'Eureka! Aha, this is precisely what Guruji had said!' Thus I have planted the seed and can only hope that someday this grows into a sturdy tree. But you will also have to do your bit by nourishing it with the fertiliser of *sādhanā* and giving it the sunshine of your heartfelt prayers.

ABOUT THE AUTHOR
Anandmurti Gurumaa

Anandmurti Gurumaa is a contemporary master guiding millions around the world towards their spiritual growth. She is an exquisite synthesis of love & wisdom. Out of sheer compassion she has been bestowing upon people the greatest gift ever viz. guiding them from the dark bondage of ignorance to the effulgence of liberating knowledge. She puts emphasis on keenly understanding the mind and persistently pursuing the practices to transcend it. Her insightful talks unravel the depths of esoteric wisdom with awe-inspiring lucidity, thereby demystifying their inherent meanings, so as to guide the path of seekers. They aim to eradicate ignorance which is the root cause of suffering.

Talking about life, Gurumaa says, "Life is simple. We complicate it." Giving a new perspective to meditation, she says, "Meditation is not contemplation. Meditation is not concentration. Meditation is a state of being." Answering questions on several such topics Gurumaa has brought about fresh insight into the understanding of these, so as to unclutter the cluttered mind of modern-day man. Her teachings lead to clarity of mind, facilitate harmonious living and show the way to rise above mundane lifestyle. Most importantly, they make one aware of that dimension of life about which one is generally oblivious.

She has extensively spoken on plethora of topics viz. life, mind, meditation, God, love, truth, relationships etc. With her characteristic humility, Anandmurti Gurumaa says, "I have nothing new to offer in terms of words, but much to offer in terms of the

Karma Unravelled

essence of truth." She has given erudite commentaries on ancient scriptures including Srimad Bhagavad Gita, Sri Guru Gita, and Gurbani, to name but a few! She has devised numerous techniques to aid meditation, written several books of immense wisdom and given remarkably in-depth eloquent discourses on numerous sages from diverse backgrounds, from different parts of India and oversees – then whether it is the Sikh Gurus or Buddha, Kabir or Rumi, Meerabai or Sahajobai, Sufi mystics or the Zen masters.

Anandmurti Gurumaa is based at her Ashram in Gannaur (Sonepat, Haryana) and is also accessible through the website www.gurumaa.com. In addition to this, Gurumaa travels all around the world to share the light of wisdom and offer an opportunity to evolve and attain the heights of spirituality. One such opportunity is a meditation retreat with the master which is held from time to time at different places across the globe. These retreats offer a perfect climate to learn various sacred techniques which rishis of ancient times taught only the select few. Besides discourse and meditation sessions, these retreats also include yoga sessions aiming to accelerate the spiritual growth of the participants.

What's more, being the compassionate Philanthropist that she is, she actively spearheads a noble endeavour called Mission Shakti which is aimed at empowering girls and women and combating the heinous practice of female foeticide which is shamefully still rampant in India.

An awakened being, a spiritual master, a rationalist, a visionary, a philosopher, a philanthropist – this may mistakenly invoke an image of a person with grave and austere disposition. But one couldn't be more wrong! A prolific poet, singer and composer; a delightful orator, contemporary and liberal; a sparkling sense of humour and a certain je ne sais quoi marks this utmost unique and endearing persona named Anandmurti Gurumaa.

It is simply not possible to be in her presence and not feel her love, her compassion, her wisdom. Her very aura imparts a sense of wellbeing, peace and contentment which has to be experienced to be believed.

Connect with the master one-on-one

Twitter
www.twitter.com/GurumaaAshram

Facebook
www.facebook.com/GurumaaAshram

Audio & video collection of
Discourse / meditation / sufi / new age / devotional music
by Anandmurti Gurumaa

Hindi Discourses

1. Astitva Se Mulaqaat (6 DVD Set)
2. Buddha Sutra (VCD)
3. Guru Ke Gyana Ka Adhikaari Kaun (2 ACD Set)
4. Ibadat (DVD)
5. Jashn-e-Kabir (3 DVD Set)
6. Kabir - The Maverick Mystic (12 DVD Set)
7. Kaisi Aarti Hoye (2 VCD Set)
8. Krishna Premanjali (6 DVD Set)
9. Kya Hai Sadhuta (VCD)
10. Mann Ka Satvik Ahaar (VCD)
11. Manotantra Vigyan (VCD)
12. Rasiya Sang Rang Barse (6 DVD Set)
13. Shankaracharya Bhaja Govindam (28 VCD Set)
14. Shivoham (30 VCD Set)
15. Shri Guru Gita (25 DVD Set)
16. Shrimad Bhagavad Gita (136 VCD Set/71 DVD Set)
17. Sri Sukhmani Sahib (25 DVD Set)
18. Teesra Kinara (DVD)
19. Tu To Mann Ke Mool Mein (VCD)
20. Anandoham (DVD)
21. Panchkosha Vigyaan (2 DVD Set)
22. Shri Ram Lakshman Samvaad (3 DVD Set)
23. Yaari Sahib (3 DVD Set)

Punjabi Discourses

1. Anand Sahib (2 ACD Set)
2. Chaupai Sahib (3 ACD Set)
3. Dil Wich Rab Disda (4 DVD Set)
4. Rang Pyar De (3 DVD Set)

English Discourses

1. God: Mystery Or Reality (VCD)
2. Know Your Mind (VCD)
3. Secrets Of Mantra, Breathing & Initiation (DVD)
4. Sutras For Healthy & Stress-Free Living (DVD)
5. Understanding The Mechanisms Of Body & Mind (DVD)
6. Awakening To The True Purpose Of Life (DVD)

MP3

1. Baba Bulle Shah (2 MP3 Set)
2. Jaap Sahib (2 MP3 Set)
3. Japji Sahib (2 MP3 Set)
4. Rehras Sahib (2 MP3 Set)
5. Salok Mahalla Novan (2 MP3 Set)
6. Shankaracharya - Bhaja Govindam (3 MP3 Set)
7. Shivoham (3 MP3 Set)
8. Shrimad Bhagavad Gita (16 MP3 Set)

Meditation

1. Beyond Boundaries/ Nishkriya Dhyana English/Hindi (ACD)
2. Breathing Winds – Hindi (ACD)
3. Hu - The Zikr (ACD)
4. Mool Mantra - Punjabi (ACD)
5. Mudra-Bhava Dhyana Eng/Hindi (ACD)
6. Odyssey of Love (Meditation Music)

7. Pranav-Omkar Dhyana Eng/Hindi (ACD)
8. Ram Ras-Sankirtan – Hindi (ACD)
9. Sacred Spaces – Hindi (ACD)
10. Shwason Ka Vigyan – Hindi (VCD)
11. Sparsh – Hindi (VCD)
12. Stuti Sutra – Hindi (ACD)
13. Tratak – Hindi (ACD)
14. Urja-Sakriya Dhyana – Eng/Hindi (ACD)
15. Waheguru Mantra (ACD)
16. Yog Nidra Eng/Hindi/Spanish (ACD)
17. Yog Nidra-Level II Hindi (ACD)
18. Yog Nidra For Youth Hindi (ACD)
19. Zikr – Call of a Sufi (ACD)
20. Rumi - Love At Its Zenith (ACD)
21. Saajanra (VCD)
22. Saanwal Saanwal (ACD)
23. Sajda (ACD)
24. Samarpan (ACD)
25. Sheikh Farid (ACD)
26. Shiv Namonkar (ACD)
27. Shiva's Ecstasy (ACD)
28. Shivoham (2 ACD Set)
29. Shoonya (ACD)
30. Shri Rama Stuti (ACD)
31. Suno Suno Meri Aawaaz (ACD)
32. Waheguru Jaap (ACD)

Devotional & Mantra Chanting

1. Aanando (ACD)
2. Ananda Stotras (ACD)
3. Anhad (ACD)
4. Avadhoo (ACD)
5. Baawari Jogan (ACD)
6. Chamkan Taare (ACD)
7. Chants of Krishna (ACD)
8. Des Begana Hai (ACD)
9. Dilbar Ki Karda-Baba Bulle Shah (2 VCD Set)
10. Fragrance Of Love (ACD)
11. Gayatri Mantra (ACD)
12. Guru Meri Pooja (ACD)
13. Ishq Hi Maula (ACD)
14. Kahe Kabira (2 ACD Set)
15. Kripa (ACD)
16. Maha Mrityunjaya (ACD)
17. Nanak Aaya (ACD)
18. Nataraja (ACD)
19. Rangi Re (ACD)

Books of Wisdom By Anandmurti Gurumaa

These books are transcriptions of the extempore talks given by Anandmurti Gurumaa from time to time at various places.

1. Anhad Ki Dhun Pyari (Hindi)
2. Antar Drishti (Hindi)
3. Antar Ke Pat Khol (Hindi, Gujrati)
4. Ath Kahe Narad (Hindi)
5. Atma Bodh (Hindi, Marathi, Telugu, Gujrati)
6. Bhaja Govindam (Hindi)
7. Chinmaya Ki Aur (Hindi)
8. Dhamma - Jeevan Aadhar (Hindi)
9. Going Beyond The Mind (English)
10. Govind Naam Mere Pran (Hindi)
11. Govind Rasdhara (Hindi)
12. Gyan Kshitij (Hindi)
13. Health & Healing Through Yoga (English)
14. In Quest Of Sadguru (English)
15. Kabira Ram Yu Sumiriye (Hindi)
16. Karuna Hridya (Hindi)
17. Know Thyself (English)
18. Mind Undressed (English)
19. Mann Ke Paar (Hindi)
20. Naame Ke Swami Har Ghat Base (Hindi)
21. Prem Deewani Meera (Hindi)
22. Prem Ka Chhalakta Jaam (Hindi)
23. Prema Bhakti Ek Utsav (Hindi)
24. Quotes Of The Unquotable (English)
25. Rehras Sahib (Punjabi)
26. Rumi Aur Main (Hindi)
27. Rumi's Love Affair (English)
28. Sadguru Kaun (Hindi)
29. Sadguru Pura Paayo (Hindi, Punjabi, Gujrati)
30. Sadhana Path: The Seeker's Companion (Dairy)
31. Shakti (English, Hindi, Gujrati, Telugu)
32. Shivoham (Hindi)
33. Sutras For Transcending Indulgence (English)
34. The Compassionate Buddha (English)
35. Truth Exposed (English)
36. Vasna Se Upramta (Hindi)
37. Yoga Se Arogya (Hindi)
38. Yuktahaar (Hindi, Telugu)

Comics

1. Toyo – A wonderful Story (English)
2. Toyo – Ek Dilchasp Kahani (Hindi)
3. Millie – I am a Girl (English)
4. Millie – Main Ek Ladki Hoon (Hindi)

To know more about the Books & CDs or to buy them online, visit www.gurumaa.com or call 09896263821/0130-221500/501

RISHI CHAITANYA ASHRAM

Energy-field for your conscious evolution

Just as flowers need the right climate, the right care to bloom and blossom, so do we need a conducive environment and guidance to evolve our consciousness and tread the path of emancipation. Presence and guidance of the master is essential on this path, as it is the master who dispels the darkness of ages and awakens the eternal light within the seeker, by sharing his own fiery light of wisdom. For this journey from unconsciousness to consciousness, from periphery to the centre, from illusion to reality, abode of the revered master Anandmurti Gurumaa, offers the perfect climate.

A hub of an immense positive energy, Rishi Chaitanya Ashram is a panacea for the modern world, blinded by storms of lust, greed, attachment, ego - all get respite and relief once they arrive in the Ashram and work towards their evolution. It is a cosmic field of energy - energy that acts as a catalyst for self-realisation. It is an energy-field where under the guidance of Gurumaa, seekers explore the inner world, understand the mechanism of mind and consciously strive to realise their true nature.

ℭ Retreats in Ashram

Retreats are the time to treat yourself with meditation, yoga, solitude, wisdom and a lot more in the evolutionary ambiance of the Ashram with the revered master Anandmurti Gurumaa. There are many opportunities to participate in the retreats which are organised around the year. Their details are published in the monthly magazine of the Ashram, Rishi Amrit and online at www.gurumaa.com.

ℭ Stay at Ashram

Stay at Rishi Chaitanya Ashram is a unique experience. It offers a simple, uncomplicated and spiritually rich environment. Rooms may be reserved by phone, via e-mail, or online at www.gurumaa.com. A minimum 15-days advance booking is required. Call 0130-2216500, 2216501, 09896263821 or e-mail your room booking request at info@gurumaa.com. For more details, visit www.gurumaa.com

ℭ Location

Located at Gannaur, District Sonepat, Haryana, Rishi Chaitanya Ashram is about 65 kms from Delhi I.S.B.T. (Inter State Bus Terminus) on National Highway 1. Seekers from all faiths are welcome to the ashram, where group meditation, solitary silence, prayer, yoga and silent contemplation are practiced.

gurumaa.com

all-new
gurumaa.com

Keeping you connected with the master in a new way...

- ✍ Watch Online Discourses & Exclusive Videos
- ✍ Read and go on reading insightful articles in Online Library
- ✍ Explore, buy and download from Online Store of Books & CDs
- ✍ Subscribe to monthly magazine from Rishi Chaitanya Ashram
- ✍ Stay updated with upcoming events & programs
- ✍ Register for retreats and workshops
- ✍ Be part of mission Shakti, an initiative to educate and empower the girl child
- ✍ Contribute online

connect. contemplate. catalyse your evolution

HINDI-ENGLISH
MONTHLY MAGAZINE
FROM RISHI CHAITANYA ASHRAM

RISHI AMRIT
Inspiring Revolution In Human Consciousness

Insight

- Dhyana Sutras
- Exclusive Articles Based On Anandmurti Gurumaa's Discourses
- Scientific Revelations For Spiritual Evolution
- Events & Programs in Ashram
- Details Of Meditation Retreats
- And much more…

To help you soar higher in inner sky…

To subscribe log on to www.gurumaa.com
Or call 09896263821 / 0130 2216500-01

Empowering the girl child

"No achievement is out of bounds for a girl.
All she needs is an opportunity. Shakti offers
this opportunity to the girl child."
Anandmurti Gurumaa

Shakti is a non-sectarian, non-political and
nondiscriminatory organisation dedicated to
empowering underprivileged girls, so that they
can lead a dignified life with financial
independence and actuate their inherent
potential. Since its inception in 1999, Shakti has
helped educate over 12,600 girls and empowered
over 2600 girls with vocational training courses.

You can support Shakti in various ways.
For more details, please visit us at
www.missionshakti.org

Notes

Notes

Notes